The Doctoral Student's Advisor and Mentor

Sage Advice from the Experts

Edited by
Raymond L. Calabrese
Page A. Smith

Rowman & Littlefield Education
A division of
ROWMAN & LITTLEFIELD PUBLISHERS, INC.
Lanham • New York • Toronto • Plymouth, UK

Published by Rowman & Littlefield Education
A division of Rowman & Littlefield Publishers, Inc.
A wholly owned subsidiary of The Rowman & Littlefield Publishing Group, Inc.
4501 Forbes Boulevard, Suite 200, Lanham, Maryland 20706
http://www.rowmaneducation.com

Estover Road, Plymouth PL6 7PY, United Kingdom

Copyright © 2010 by Raymond L. Calabrese and Page A. Smith

All rights reserved. No part of this book may be reproduced in any form or by any electronic or mechanical means, including information storage and retrieval systems, without written permission from the publisher, except by a reviewer who may quote passages in a review.

British Library Cataloguing in Publication Information Available

Library of Congress Cataloging-in-Publication Data
Library of Congress Cataloging-in-Publication Data

The doctoral student's advisor and mentor : sage advice from the experts / edited by Raymond L. Calabrese, Page A. Smith.
　　p. cm.
　Includes bibliographical references.
　ISBN 978-1-60709-449-4 (cloth : alk. paper) — ISBN 978-1-60709-450-0 (pbk. : alk. paper) — ISBN 978-1-60709-451-7 (ebook)
　1. Doctor of philosophy degree—United States. 2. Doctoral students—United States. 3. Mentoring in education—United States. 4. Faculty advisors—United States. I. Calabrese, Raymond L., 1942- II. Smith, Page A., 1953-
　LB2386.D625 2010
　378.2—dc22
　　　　　　　　　　　　　　　　　　　　　　　　　　　　2010012009

∞ ™ The paper used in this publication meets the minimum requirements of American National Standard for Information Sciences—Permanence of Paper for Printed Library Materials, ANSI/NISO Z39.48-1992.

Printed in the United States of America

To Barbara Hampton Calabrese—BFF

and

Professor Sally J. Zepeda—A Good Friend and Colleague

—Ray

To Trish—Her Stamina Dwarfs Anything I Can Muster

—Page

To Barbara Hampton Calabrese—BFF

and

Professor Sally J. Zepeda—A Good Friend and Colleague

—Ray

To Trish—Her Stamina Dwarfs Anything I Can Muster

—Page

Contents

Acknowledgments		ix
Introduction		xi
Part I	**Strategies for Beginning the Doctoral Program**	1
1	Starting the Doctoral Process Dr. James E. Henderson, Duquesne University School of Education	3
2	Ten Suggestions When Starting the Doctoral Process: You Are Still a Person, Too, Aren't You? Dr. H. Richard Milner IV, Vanderbilt University, and Dr. Judson Laughter, The University of Tennessee, Knoxville	13
3	Thinking About Starting a Doctoral Program? Plan Ahead for Success Dr. Patti L. Chance, San Diego State University	21
4	Life in the Fast Lane: Beginning the Doctoral Process Dr. Page Smith, University of Texas–San Antonio	27
5	Beginning the Doctoral Journey Dr. Pamela A. Angelle, The University of Tennessee	31

6	Considerations at the Threshold: The Beginning of Doctoral Studies María Luisa González, University of Texas–El Paso	37
7	Just Beginning a Doctoral Program? Dr. CarolAnne M. Kardash, University of Nevada–Las Vegas, and Dr. Jeanne T. Amlund, Pennsylvania State University, Greater Allegheny	41
8	You're Sure You Really Want to Do This? Dr. Stephen Jacobson, University at Buffalo–State University of New York	47

Part II Conquering Common Doctoral Challenges: Motivation, Procrastination, and Reenergizing 51

9	Getting Over the "ABD" Hump: The Secret Is Avoiding Procrastination Dr. Bruce W. Tuckman, The Ohio State University	53
10	Avoid Being Labeled ABD Dr. Stacey Edmonson, Sam Houston State University	57
11	When Motivation Hits Bottom Dr. Connie L. Fulmer, University of Colorado–Denver	63
12	Passion: Don't Embark Without It Dr. Megan Tschannen-Moran, The College of William and Mary	67
13	Brains, Heart, Courage, and Home: When Doctoral Students Have Significant Personal Issues Confounding the Completion of the Dissertation Dr. Patrick D. Pauken, Bowling Green State University	71

Part III Reducing, Coping, and Preventing Stress 79

14	Managing Your Stress Dr. Betty Merchant, University of Texas–San Antonio	81

15 Eliminate Political Tensions With Your Dissertation
Committee and Major Professor 85
Dr. Mary Frances Agnello, Texas Tech University

16 Life Happens: So What Do I Do Now? 91
Dr. Rosemary S. Caffarella, Cornell University

17 Helping a Graduate Student Develop Self-Directedness
in Stressful Times: A Brief Conversation 97
Dr. Mark A. Gooden, University of Texas–Austin

18 Preparing for Qualifying Examinations 103
Dr. A. William Place, University of Dayton

Part IV **Life After the Doctorate: Opportunities for Advancing Your Career** 107

19 Using Your Dissertation as a Steppingstone to
a University Faculty Position 109
Dr. Michelle D. Young, University of Texas–Austin

20 Using the Dissertation as a Vehicle for Publishing:
A Conversation Between Professor and Doctoral Student 117
*Dr. Charles L. Slater, California State University–
Long Beach, and Mtra. Gema López Gorosave,
Escuela Normal Estatal in Ensenada, B.C., México*

21 Maximizing Your Dissertation to Propel Your Career 127
Dr. George Theoharis, Syracuse University

22 What Do You Want to Do With This?
Means-Driven Dissertation Writing 131
Dr. Catherine Lugg, Rutgers, State University of New Jersey

Final Thoughts 135

Biographies 137

Acknowledgments

As editors of *The Doctoral Student's Advisor and Mentor: Sage Advice From the Experts*, we are indebted to the 25 professors and dissertation advisors from the most prestigious universities in the United States for taking time from their demanding schedules to contribute to this book. The book is a product of their collective wisdom, passion, and experience linked to mentoring doctoral students. They provided us with significant hope for the future of doctoral education in the United States.

We acknowledge Dr. Thomas F. Koerner, editor for Rowman & Littlefield Education. The core of this book is mentoring. Tom is the exemplar of an exceptional mentor. We appreciate and acknowledge his mentoring throughout this project. One of the editors of this book has been fortunate to have had Tom as a mentor for several years. This mentoring relationship began when the editor was a middle school and high school principal and Tom was the executive director for the National Association of Secondary School Principals. Like the stories in this book, this mentoring relationship continues.

Introduction

The core of this book focuses on utilizing the power of faculty mentoring to empower doctoral students to complete their doctoral studies successfully. For doctoral students, a mentor is a person who points toward the goal, helping them chart a course to advance their careers. For the mentor, it is a means of *paying it forward*, helping doctoral students to become self-sufficient contributors to society. Mentoring centers around several aspects: the relationship is reciprocal, caring, and transforming (Healy & Welchert, 1990).

Homer's *Odyssey* gives us the story of Mentor. Mentor acts as a teacher and guardian of Odysseus's son Telemachus while Odysseus goes to battle in the Trojan War. The concept of mentoring originates in Greek mythology and continues to the present. A mentor takes on many roles: advisor, teacher, guide, or friend. In each case, mentoring involves a relationship between the teacher and the person being taught or guided. The mentor has an investment in the emotional, intellectual, and spiritual development of the person he or she chooses to mentor. The mentor operates with a belief that the mentee is worthy of the time and emotional investment and that the investment will pay dividends to society by becoming a force for good through the mentee's contributions.

In contemporary professional academic settings, one way mentoring is observed is through the relationship between a major professor and his or her doctoral student. This relationship is complex. When flourishing, the mentoring relationship fortifies and advances the doctoral student's inherent capacity for achievement. The mentoring relationship, at its best, is a core component of intellectual, psychological, and emotional growth for the mentee as well as a benefit for the mentor (Barondess, 1997).

As editors of the book, we strongly believe that mentoring is a central component of any doctoral program. We thought of the importance of faculty as mentors and how they enhance the careers of doctoral students. We agree with the concept put forth by Johnson (2007) that a mentor provides the mentee with knowledge, guidance, encouragement, and challenges in the quest of becoming a full member of the mentor's profession. As our thinking progressed, the genesis of an idea formed: What would it be like for a doctoral student to get advice from a mentor on any aspect of the doctoral process at a time and place when he or she needed it most? What would it be like if exceptional faculty from universities throughout the United States provided sage advice for students? We believed that doctoral students would benefit immensely. We also believed faculty, who serve as major professors or advisors, would benefit from the insights of their colleagues across the country.

EDITOR'S NOTE TO DOCTORAL STUDENTS

This collection of mentoring chapters showcases 25 professors and dissertation advisors from the most prestigious universities in the United States. They give you an extraordinary range of mentoring advice that speaks directly to you. They answer the timeless question: How do I get my doctorate? You receive exactly the advice you need. You discover clues to complete your doctoral journey.

This book is filled with encouragement. You can flip through the chapters to select an area of interest. Whether you are just beginning to think about entering a doctoral program, presently taking course studies, under stress, or don't know what your future could offer, this is an ideal book for you because it maps the entire doctoral process.

Each chapter addresses a professional or personal component of the doctoral process that represents how these exceptional faculty best mentor their doctoral students. Faculty contributions exemplify diverse perspectives of mentoring: (a) Some faculty are direct and forthright, pointing the mentee toward his or her destination; (b) some faculty share personal experiences—offering mentoring advice from the perspective of someone who traveled a similar path; and (c) some faculty structure a dialogue between the faculty as mentor and you as the doctoral student. In all cases, they open possibilities for achieving success in doctoral studies.

Faculty contributions are divided into three mentoring areas: (1) Strategies for Beginning the Doctoral Program; (2) Conquering Common Doctoral Challenges: Motivation, Procrastination, and Reenergizing; and (3) Reducing, Coping, and Preventing Stress.

As editors, we are honored to have our names on this remarkable mentoring book that you are about to read. We hope you uncover the secrets that will make you successful and advance your career.

REFERENCES

Barondess, J. (1997). On mentoring. *Journal of the Royal Society of Medicine, 90*(June), 347–349.

Healy, C. C., & Welchert, J. (1990). Mentoring relations: A definition to advance research and practice. *Educational Researcher, 19*(9), 17–21.

Johnson, W. B. (2007). Transformational supervision: When supervisors mentor. *Professional Psychology: Research and Practice, 38*(3), 259–267.

1

STRATEGIES FOR BEGINNING THE DOCTORAL PROGRAM

This section of *The Doctoral Student's Advisor and Mentor* is dedicated to "Starting the Doctoral Process." The mentoring advice offered by our contributors speaks specifically to beginning the doctoral process, having a strategic plan for success, and establishing effective work habits.

- Dr. James E. Henderson: Starting the Doctoral Process
- Drs. H. Richard Milner IV and Judson Laughter: Ten Suggestions When Starting the Doctoral Process: You Are Still a Person, Too, Aren't You?
- Dr. Pattie L. Chance: Thinking About Starting a Doctoral Program? Plan Ahead for Success.
- Dr. Page Smith: Life in the Fast Lane: Beginning the Doctoral Process
- Dr. Pamela A. Angelle: Beginning the Doctoral Journey
- Dr. María Luisa González: Considerations at the Threshold: The Beginning of Doctoral Studies
- Drs. CarolAnne M. Kardash and Jeanne T. Amlund: Just Beginning a Doctoral Program?
- Dr. Stephen Jacobson: You're Sure You Really Want to Do This?

1

Starting the Doctoral Process

Dr. James E. Henderson
Duquesne University School of Education

So you're just starting a doctoral program and that program has a capstone requirement of a dissertation. Well, then, let's begin preparing you right away for that experience so you won't begin like I and so many other doctoral students began the doctoral process. To say that I was clueless regarding the dissertation when I began my doctoral work would be putting it mildly. That cluelessness may have, of course, contributed to the 3-plus years it took me to finish my dissertation after I had finished coursework. Let's not have you fall into the same trap.

I'm now into my 18th year of working with doctoral students, and I've chaired and been a member of scores of dissertation committees. Some of the advice I'm going to give you is born of those experiences. Much of the advice contained in this chapter, though, comes directly from many of the successful graduates of the doctoral program I direct. It's their wisdom and insight that will work for you. I'm going to focus on four main topic areas: Establishing and Maintaining a Productive Process; Selecting a Topic; Attitude; and "Auditioning" and Selecting Your Dissertation Committee. Let's get started.

ESTABLISHING AND MAINTAINING A PRODUCTIVE PROCESS

I'll bet that you're excited to begin your journey as a doctoral student. That's great. As former world-class runner Jim Ryun said though, "Motivation is what gets you started. Habit is what keeps you going." Let's help you build profitable habits that will lead not only to success during your coursework, but to dissertation completion.

Several of my former students reported that the most important mental practice was to look at one small task at a time—focus on that task, finish it, and then move on. One graduate likened it to "taking small bites of the dissertation, but to keep chewing throughout the process; a spin-off of the 'how to eat an elephant' philosophy . . . one bite at a time."

Another graduate wisely advised: "Set short terms goals—don't start by looking at the end, look at the process to get to the end and take 2-week chunks at a time. Set goals for how many articles and books you will read and/or the pages you will write for 2-week periods. Stick to your goals, but don't beat yourself up if you don't make it for one of the 2-week periods."

One more graduate amplified that approach by stating: "During our first informational meeting I was told to create a schedule and follow it like a job. That piece of advice resonated with me and grounded me when I would get off track. When I found myself not making progress, the first thing I would do is schedule my workload. I would set the time I would work and one or two goals for that time. That persistence of scheduling helped me finish while going through two jobs changes and a move of several thousand miles."

Another graduate underscored the importance of a schedule: "Write every day. Include writing as part of your daily routine . . . just like brushing your teeth. Schedule it for 1 or 2 hours each day and give yourself 2 days off each week. No excuses . . . just do it!"

Finally, another graduate scheduled her anticipated dissertation defense while she was still in her first doctoral class: "My advice that I have given to many, per Steven Covey, is to 'begin with the end in mind.' Make a conscious decision as to when you want to defend your dissertation. Put it on a calendar and work backwards to develop all of the 'due dates' along the way. Obviously, there may be some modifications necessary, but a written plan with specific actions and timelines will keep you focused on completion. It may require some 'all nighters,' but in the end, it will be worth it!" In fact, one graduate reported having purchased her doctoral cap and gown during her first semester and, while she grumbled about the cost (they are expensive!), she reported having effectively burned the dreaded bridges of ABD (All But Dissertation)—she was committed to finishing.

You will be well served to determine the time during the day, week, month, and semester/quarter when you're most productive and schedule your doctoral work accordingly. Not one plan works for everyone; you certainly have to know your strengths and work style. This graduate did: "I was not good at designating an hour or two a day, like some people do. I had to devote consecutive days, because I am one who needs to stay on the same train of thought. So for me, the month of December was the key. I took vacation days and sent the family out shopping between Christmas and New Year's to get my work done. My son had gotten a dart board for Christmas that year. So I would write for about 2 hours, and then go and throw darts for 30 minutes. I'm not sure that method would be recommended for everyone, but it worked for me." The advice to work according to what allows you to be productive will serve you well in both courses and, ultimately, in dissertation completion.

Distraction is an issue after coursework and entering the dissertation stage. Knowing himself, one graduate summed that up: "The best piece of advice for me was simple . . . don't work at home or at the office. You will always find something else to work on and contribute to the procrastination process! Someone else referred to it as 'cleaning your gutters.' All of a sudden the thing that you hate doing the most around the house becomes your favorite chore. Get away from home and the office. Find a location that is neutral—a place where you can do nothing else but work on your coursework and, ultimately, your dissertation."

If you absolutely cannot find a place to work other than your home or office, take this graduate's story to heart: "I wanted to find a place to do the writing where I wouldn't be disturbed. In my house, there are few options and I actually considered renting an office space—too much money. I was on my way out the door to purchase a 'shed' that I was going to put in the backyard and convert into an office—my wife talked me back into reality on that one as well! What I finally did was convert the dormer in my bedroom into my office." You may think you can handle distractions, but it is so easy to procrastinate—don't put yourself in temptation's way.

Organizing your efforts in an efficient and effective manner is vital. One successful doctoral student noted: "Keep a comprehensive filing system for all research examined . . . either by paper filing or eFiling in coded folders. This was invaluable advice, and I am still referring to these sources. This organization made the process so much easier." Moreover—and we'll talk a bit more about this later in "Selecting a Topic"—organize your efforts right from the beginning to build your Chapter 2, your Literature Review: "When doing assignments, focus papers, and projects to the general area of your anticipated research. This increases the reading related to your area and for your literature review."

Disciplined and focused effort is required and reading—lots of reading—is essential as one graduate noted: "READ, READ, READ! Reading presents various perspectives of your topic. Read outside of your normal interest area. This can present a new and fresh perspective to your topic. Read contradictory opinions to your view. This will help strengthen your perspective or change it all together. Read, Read, Read. Enough said here. You can never say enough about reading. Take notes on relevant readings. Keep ALL of your notes related to readings. You cannot remember everything you have read."

The last bit or process advice sounds hard, but it's terribly important. A graduate who went through some personal ordeals during her doctoral program summed it up: "Put your life on hold while you go through this. You cannot complete a doctorate by fitting it into the cracks in your life. It has to be a major priority if you are going to complete the degree. I didn't give up everything but I did cut back on my personal activities for the years I was in the program. It helped tremendously to just be able to concentrate on the coursework and writing." While this approach requires you to delay certain gratifications, it truly works.

SELECTING A TOPIC

The noted scholar and sometimes basketball coach Pat Riley once noted, "Look for your choices, pick the best one, then go with it." That's excellent advice for a doctoral student, even and especially near the beginning of your program. Much conventional wisdom holds that you shouldn't lock into a topic, or even a general area of research interest, until you've completed quite a bit of coursework and done a lot of reading. Literally every one of my successful doctoral students, though, indicated the importance of the advice to select a topic area early, though some had slightly different perspectives on this counsel.

One reason dealt with passion. As one graduate noted: "The best piece of advice I got was choose a topic that is close to your heart—this was good advice because you eat, drink, and sleep (or not!) your topic for months. If you are not truly passionate about it, loss of interest could occur." Another amplified on this suggestion: "Find a topic early in the process you can sink your teeth into for your dissertation. It needs to be an area that motivates you and is reasonable and meaningful in the scope to do the research. If you need help finding a topic, you can contact doctoral students who completed their dissertations. Ideas for a dissertation seem to come more easily after someone has struggled through the entire process."

Finally, one successful student affirmed: "As I began the process, many people told me to pick a topic that had interest to me personally. That was the best piece of advice that was given to me. Since I followed that advice, not only did I finish, I really enjoyed working on my project. Had I picked something that was not as interesting, I probably would have taken much longer. Some of my colleagues just picked topics that they thought would get them finished, and they did not get as much out of the process as I did."

Determining your tentative area of research interest enables you to "build" your dissertation—especially your Introduction and Literature Review (typically Chapters 1 and 2)—during your doctoral coursework. One graduate recommended: "Pick a topic that you are interested in and stick to that topic throughout the program. Make sure that every paper you write and everything you read is somehow related to the topic. I did this and it really worked. The topic was originally broad, but as time went on I began to have a focus and a dissertation topic."

Another graduate stated: "Choose your topic at the get go and stick with it . . . AND . . . in every class, complete the assignments with your dissertation in mind." Finally, a newly-minted doctor affirmed: "This advice was good because at the end of my coursework, while my colleagues were just about to embark on their dissertation topic and research, my dissertation Chapters 1 and 2 were completed. I could see the light at the end of the tunnel!"

Finally, passion and interest are important, but flexibility along the way is vital. One graduate's story is illustrative: "My advice would be to start with your passion in mind—you don't want to put countless hours of reading and research into something that just doesn't stimulate you—but be willing to work with your advisors to massage your ideas so that you can develop good research questions or alternate research ideas that are TIED to your passion (or you find another passion along the way). I thought my passion was kindergarten programming in a kindergarten-only building. But, when I sat with an expert on qualitative research and told him why I had this passion, he was able to pull out that my real passion was collaborative environments. This allowed me to focus on my passion and to still use the kindergarten-only building as the site of my case study."

Another graduate acknowledged: "Even if you don't know the particular research questions, having an idea of the topic greatly helped me to focus on the research that I could include or rule out in my research. This saved me a lot of time. I would suspect that those who defended early had a good idea of their dissertation topic early on in the program."

ATTITUDE

Thomas Foxwell Buxton once opined, "With ordinary talent and extraordinary perseverance, all things are attainable." This is by no means an attempt to denigrate your skills, talents, and abilities, but it is a reminder that you need to enter—and continue—your doctoral program with a mindset of perseverance. One of my graduates told me that "the sage advice that I received included, 'you can do this, I did it and you can, too'; this piece of advice helped to give me confidence that I would be successful in this endeavor."

A willingness to work with others is an essential attitude. Communicate with family and friends about the time required for your studies. Your family and friends are important ingredients to the success of your journey. Your time with them will be affected and they need to know that you are still there.

One graduate had to overcome some difficult personal circumstances on the journey to the doctorate: "When I began, I made up my mind that I would really discipline myself to work for several hours a day. For me, it was a bittersweet process. Some days, life would throw me a curve ball; that meant my work sat on the computer collecting dust. I was a single mother of two children and going through a horrible custody battle once again, which ended like previous custody battles, meaning the girls remained with me. The girls were with me during the school year and with their father during the summer. I had to juggle being a parent and a student at the same time—not an easy process; however, it taught me to value any time I had to work. The time that I had with the children was dedicated for them. This is how I was able to continue to work through the process without too much stalling. I learned that disciplining myself each day is important but more important is knowing when to step back and smell the roses!"

For others it wasn't their family members; it was their professional colleagues. The best advice someone gave me was not to be afraid to use other people to help me get through [the doctoral program]. 'No one does this alone,' was an oft-repeated phrase, and it was true. If I did not have various people along the way who I could count on for help, advice, and encouragement, I may never have finished. 'Everyone wants to help you,' we were told, and it was true."

As one successful doctoral student advised: "Enjoy the journey. Don't let the work, the hours required, and the sacrifice prevent you from experiencing the pure joy and excitement that the journey provides." Another reflected on her life's purpose: "I personally had a fair amount of internal struggle in deciding whether or not to take this project on at my age—I was in my late 40s and recently separated from a 25-year marriage. I certainly did not see the merits financially. After 2 weeks of severe internal searching, I finally arrived at something I now call my '85 question.' Basically, my decision to take out a school loan and complete this conquest came down to me asking the question of what regrets I would have in my life when I reached the age of 85. Clearly, not attaining my doctorate would have been one of my big regrets."

That sentiment is reinforced by another graduate who indicated: "My best advice to myself was that such decisions in life should be based on personal goals and not related to possible future salary increases, school loan debt, or any belief that this will enable you to climb to the top of the proverbial career ladder. I did it for myself. Once I mastered that thought, I knew I would have no difficultly completing the program in a timely fashion . . . and it was a wonderful adventure! It is the best advice I could offer. The decision needs to be internally driven to be committed to completion."

"AUDITIONING" AND SELECTING YOUR DISSERTATION COMMITTEE

The term "select" has several definitions that are meaningful in this last piece of advice—the selection of your dissertation committee. Here are some definitions to consider:

(superl.) Worthy of being chosen or preferred; select; superior; precious; valuable.
(superl.) Selected with care, and due attention to preference; deliberately chosen.
(n.) The thing or person chosen; that which is approved and selected in preference to others.

You may think that, since you're early into your doctoral program, thinking about the composition of your dissertation committee should be accomplished far into the future. Based on the reaction of my graduates, not to mention my own experience, you would be wrong. One graduate noted: "Begin to choose potential dissertation committee members wisely and early. Think of your interactions, especially in coursework, with faculty members as auditions or interviews. See which faculty members get back to you promptly and give you usable feedback. Look at a range of factors such as research expertise, areas of interest, demonstrated personal support, and a track record of supporting doctoral students at the dissertation level."

Another graduate identified her dissertation chair early "because she gave me specific feedback, was passionate about my topic, and we met in a timely manner." A different graduate similarly advised identifying strengths and interests early on: "The best advice I received was to choose members who have a depth of experience and to choose a chair who has served on a number of dissertation committees. The chair should have strong leadership skills to be your advocate as needed. Start thinking early regarding potential members and get to know them and their strengths well."

The importance of the chair is amplified by another graduate who learned her lesson the hard way. She noted: "I learned the hard way how vital an exemplary, experienced chair is. I chose someone who had a great personality, but was inexperienced in serving on dissertation committees and did not have a strong backbone. Thus, he was not well versed in the process and did not meet appropriate paperwork deadlines and when he needed to be a strong leader, he was not. This delayed my dream of graduating with my class." Perhaps the most succinct piece of advice for "auditioning" prospective committee members came from a graduate who suggested that you should "Only ask people to be on your committee who you wouldn't mind having over to your house for dinner." That says a lot.

SUMMARY

Let's summarize this advice in the spirit of Oliver Wendell Holmes: "I would not give a fig for the simplicity this side of complexity, but I would give my life for the simplicity on the other side of complexity." Setting yourself up early in your program for dissertation success is very important. Select a dissertation topic area (if not a specific topic itself) about which you have considerable passion and interest so you can "feed" your lit review throughout your coursework.

Establish a work process and routine early on that will allow you to shut out distractions yet deal with the exigencies of life. Maintain an attitude of perseverance and a willingness to ask for help. Choose dissertation committee members (especially your chair) who have a track record of success and who have demonstrated—to you—that they are supportive, timely, interested, and knowledgeable. Do these things and you are well on your way to dissertation success.

2

Ten Suggestions When Starting the Doctoral Process: You Are Still a Person, Too, Aren't You?

Dr. H. Richard Milner IV
Vanderbilt University

Dr. Judson Laughter
The University of Tennessee, Knoxville

In this chapter, we provide advice, in an informal manner, to readers just starting their doctoral studies. The story of your doctoral studies will be inundated and nuanced with ebbs and flows. There will be times when you will feel the most excited and confident you have ever felt. Conversely, there will be times when you feel inadequate, unconfident, and incapable of success in your program. Rest assured—the emotional and psychological variance you experience is normal. Even the most successful doctoral students and graduates have described times when they felt and believed that they were not capable of success in a doctoral program.

What we provide below are 10 suggestions for those beginning the doctoral process—some philosophical and others more practical but all interrelated. The suggestions represent what we believe to be essential for success in a doctoral program. At the heart of the suggestions is the idea that your identity is closely linked to your experiences and success in a doctoral program. Your ability to navigate your doctoral program successfully is inextricably tied to your evolving and developing (professional) identity, a point on which we elaborate throughout this chapter.

The authors of this chapter have an important and multifaceted relationship: the first author (Milner) was the dissertation/doctoral advisor to the second author (Laughter). We believe we are well equipped to offer the advice and suggestions discussed herein because each of us has sat where readers of this chapter presently find themselves. That is, we began and completed a doctoral program at some point in the past and continue to share a relationship that at times could be seen as academic teacher/student, professional older brother/younger brother, and personal friends. The recurrent question that guided the suggestions that follow is: Based on our experiences and knowing what we know now, what would we tell doctoral students just beginning their journey?

The sections that follow are prioritized, beginning with the most important area of consideration.

DECIDE WHO YOU ARE AND WHAT YOU ARE (NOT) WILLING TO NEGOTIATE

As a first-year doctoral student, you will need to engage in deep levels of reflection about who you are, what you believe, and why you are pursuing the work you are. You may find it easiest to become what someone else wants you to become if you are not clear about your own convictions and how they converge or diverge with others' expectations and suggestions.

For instance, you may develop a relationship with a professor, become excitingly interested in his or her work, and want to design your career along a similar trajectory. Take time to reflect on any such attraction. You will be building on the work of those who came before, but you want to do something new and consistent with your worldview and belief system. Try not to hold too tightly to any preconceived notions or theoretical frameworks.

A change or adaptation in a core belief will have wide-ranging consequences for your identity and your work. See your doctoral studies as a time to stretch and grow and to build your identity more consistently with who you are and who you are becoming. We both found it useful to keep in mind the mantra: here is what I think/believe/understand, but I could be wrong!

STRIVE FOR BALANCE EARLY ON

In addition to engaging in the important identity work of deciding who you are and what you are and are not willing to negotiate, it is important for you to begin the doctoral process striving for balance in terms of your personal and professional lives and experiences. The work of a doctoral student is endless if you allow it to be. For instance, this means that if you do not decide to make or take time for exercising and maintaining a healthy lifestyle early on, it will be difficult to "reclaim" this lifestyle later.

Family members and other areas for which you are responsible and to which you are connected can easily become afterthoughts if you do not make them a priority from the outset of your doctoral studies. You can often combine the two when pressed for time; Dr. Laughter used long bike rides to listen and relisten to audio recordings of participant interviews while analyzing his dissertation data.

BE ORGANIZED AND KEEP EXCELLENT RECORDS

It will benefit you to develop solid and well-organized records and files. These files should be maintained digitally and with old-fashioned, more traditional hard copies. Take excellent notes throughout your experience and organize them in ways that allow you to build your work and to mentor others in the future. Each class, meeting, or interaction becomes part of your doctoral story, and even the most casual interaction may one day become vital to your own success or to the success of others.

Likewise, if you can decide early on what general direction you want your dissertation to take, you can bend this organization toward that project and make every course, paper, and project build to a pinnacle—one that allows you to complete the dissertation having a well-established set of documents from which to draw.

VIEW THE PROCESS AS A JOURNEY, NOT A DESTINATION

As we have talked to others who have completed doctoral programs, one theme seems constant: If they could go back to their doctoral experiences, they would enjoy the journey and not rush to complete the process. Understandably, there are outside forces that make it difficult to remain in graduate school for an extended period. With financial demands looming and luring, it can be difficult to see the process as more of a journey than a destination. However, it is essential for you to realize that you will forever be a learner in the profession and that you should find pleasure in the journey that is your story.

LAUGH AND DON'T TAKE THE PROCESS TOO SERIOUSLY

It can be difficult to "lighten up" a bit with the strain and stress of expectations, such as looming semester deadlines. The workload associated with your doctoral studies will probably seem to fluctuate, with several deadlines crashing in on you at once, only to be followed by a couple weeks of relative calm.

Although your doctoral story is unique, we doubt that you will come up against something that no one in human history has ever faced before. You may feel as if you are all alone on the raging seas, but you are not! In fact, to extend the metaphor further, what appears to be an open ocean may turn out to be only a few feet deep when you stand up, reach out, and ask for help.

Remember, the hardship and ease, the joy and the pain, are all part of your doctoral journey, and each plays a role in the development of your scholastic identity. So, it is essential that you not drive yourself nuts throughout the process. We believe that you should laugh a lot. Do not take the doctoral process so seriously that you forget to find the humor in and through your experiences.

TAKE THE PROCESS SERIOUSLY

That said, deadlines are important and should be met; coursework is important and should be taken seriously; relationships are vital and have to be nurtured. One of the worst things you can do is to get into a habit of making excuses for setbacks or failure. You may miss a deadline. You may forget about a meeting. When that happens, admit it, apologize, and work to be better. Your professors have been where you are and have probably made similar mistakes.

It is all part of the process. Likewise, your institution will have hoops through which you have to jump. They may be annoying at best or downright tyrannical at worst, but there are more productive ways to better a system than obstinacy or rudeness. Jump through the hoops and use the experience to better yourself, those around you, and whatever institution you find yourself in down the road. It is the rare dissertation that completely upends and remakes an institution or field overnight (unless your name is, say, Noam Chomsky).

DO AS MUCH READING AS YOU POSSIBLY CAN

Intimately knowing your field and those who have come before is what allows you to build on those foundations and discover untouched areas. It is important for you not only to read in your particular field but also for you to read broadly and to build on other disciplines, such as those in arts and sciences, medicine, religion, engineering, and business.

As you read, develop an understanding of what questions have been asked and answered before, and how the field came to the answers it now claims as obvious or natural. As a doctoral student, you have the opportunity to explore multiple paradigms in each course you take. Now is a great time to begin making connections between and among fields, using tools or ideas developed in one to expand or hone another.

BUILD AS MANY SKILLS AS POSSIBLE

It is essential for you to build skills that are transferable to different aspects of your work. While there is information and knowledge you will want to learn, there are many skills that you will need to acquire (e.g., organizational skills, critical and analytical thinking skills, and writing and editing skills). These skills will serve you well in the future. It is the rare academic who only does research or only advises students.

As a professional, your duties will range from research to teaching to advising to writing to reading to traveling to conferences and beyond. You should build as many skills as possible to assist you with future transitional work, particularly those that would be required if you decide to accept a position in higher education as a professor. Remember, your main duties will be associated with service, teaching, and research or scholarship.

START BUILDING MEANINGFUL RELATIONSHIPS BY NETWORKING AT CONFERENCES AND SENDING EMAILS TO INTERESTING PROFESSORS AND COLLEAGUES

Even the biggest name in your field will often make time to answer the email of a student. In fact, Dr. Milner makes it a point in many of his courses to have his students reach out and interview a "big-name researcher." You will find that many professors will give students a higher priority than their colleagues. No matter how big the name, it is always nice to hear that some new doctoral student finds your work interesting and valuable.

As a new doctoral student, go to conferences even if you are not presenting. Use your time to hear other voices and stories. Even big names are often willing to meet for coffee or a quick meal while at a conference. Just think, the professor you have coffee with during your first trip to the American Educational Research Association's annual conference may wind up chairing the search committee for a job in which you are interested 5 years later.

REMEMBER WHERE YOU CAME FROM

As much as some of us would like to deny it, the institutions where we earn our doctorates play a large role in determining our professional academic identities. Even if you fight your institution every step of the way, in many ways your department, your professors, and your cohort are developing you.

The professors and colleagues at your institution are your biggest resource when working on your dissertation, writing a paper, or even looking for a job. You want these people on your side, so go out of your way to engage and build those positive relationships. On that day when you do finish, and someday you will, do not see leaving your institution as the time or chance to bad mouth those with whom you had disagreements.

When you have disagreements or arguments, and you will, be professional and give the other party a chance to work things out. This is a lesson we are often taught in kindergarten and somehow seem to forget by the time doctoral studies come around. Play fair and your time as a doctoral student will be much happier and productive and will provide the firm foundation you need for building a career. When you reminisce in your later, tenured years, you want the memories of your doctoral studies to be some of the happiest of your life, a time when the world was opening up and you were molding an academic identity all your own.

And perhaps most importantly, regardless of how successful you are in your doctoral studies and subsequent career, remember: You Are Still a Person, Too, Aren't You? Do not lose sight of the fact that we are all human beings hoping to contribute to improving the human condition with our lives and our work!

3

Thinking About Starting a Doctoral Program? Plan Ahead for Success

Dr. Patti L. Chance
San Diego State University

When I served in the role of coordinator of a doctoral program, I often received inquiries from students about starting a doctoral program. First contacts were usually via phone or email and went something like this: "I'm interested in starting the doctoral program and need to know something about the program and how to apply." I always responded to such requests with, "Let's schedule an appointment so we can talk." A doctoral program is a huge undertaking in one's life and represents a commitment of 3 to 6 years. This is not a decision where you want to gather all your information from e-mail exchanges or Web browsing. If a potential doctoral student was unable to make a personal visit to my office, I would schedule a phone conference, so that we could spend 30 minutes to an hour of uninterrupted time.

Thus, as you read this chapter, consider yourself in the role of that potential doctoral student and take a few minutes to engage in some reflection as I outline some major items for you to think about as you embark upon this great adventure: the doctoral degree.

CONSIDER YOUR REASONS FOR PURSUING A DOCTORAL DEGREE

My first instruction to you is to think seriously about why you want a doctoral degree. There is no right or wrong answer to this question, and ultimately the answer is a personal one. It involves a decision to make a great commitment to your field. There are many good reasons to obtain this degree, but here are some questions to consider.

- Do you want to pursue a path in academia, as a professor in an institution of higher education? If so, in what kind of institution do you want to work? Do you want to focus on research in the field, or are you more interested in working in an institution predominately dedicated to teaching?
- Do you want a doctoral degree primarily for professional development, that is to provide you with knowledge or skills that will help you do your current job better or perhaps to enter into a corporate or consulting role?
- Do you want a doctoral degree solely for your own satisfaction?
- Are you unsure of your long-term goals and simply want this degree for future doors it might open?

How you answer these questions will help you find the right program for you. If you are interested in academia, will the program you are considering provide you with opportunities to do research with professors who are known in the field? Will you have occasions to make presentations or publish with the faculty? Even if you think that you don't want to do research at a university or other institution, but instead want to teach, you should seriously consider the preparation you will receive in your doctoral program to design and conduct research. Most institutions of higher education, including small liberal arts colleges and regional colleges and universities, expect their faculty to do some research and publishing.

Consider whether this is the absolutely right program and field of study for your goals. For the most part, institutions of higher education expect faculty to have degrees that specifically match the discipline in which they hold a position. This may sound like an obvious statement, but it isn't always that simple. For instance, in my field of educational leadership, I often have inquiries from people who want to enter the professoriate to work with pre-service teachers. If that is what they really want to do, I suggest they pursue a doctoral degree in teacher education or a specific education field such as elementary education, because a degree in educational leadership will be focused on organizational and leadership development, not teacher education.

The same might be true in more traditional disciplines such as the sciences, especially if your research interest spans across disciplines. For example, plant ecology and microbiology are two separate fields of study that intersect, yet are often not integrated into a single degree. Carefully considering the right path for one's goal is important. When interests overlap, which degree program provides a better fit, or are there ways to combine the two?

In some instances, a person may choose a doctoral degree outside his or her academic area. A good example of this is the person with a master's degree in mathematics who is teaching at a community college and has interest in continuing at the community college as a department chair, dean, or other administrator. This person may choose a doctoral degree in higher education administration instead of mathematics.

The previous scenario crosses into the area of professional development or job movement or promotion. If you are planning to develop yourself within the corporate world or as a private consultant, what are the skills and credentials you will need? Chances are, even if you are not primarily a researcher, you will be writing professionally. Thus, looking at a program that will help develop your skills as both a researcher and as a consumer of research will be important. Further, what credentials will the institutions that hire you expect? Is the reputation of the university or of the faculty with whom you study important?

Finally, no matter what your reason for pursuing a doctoral degree: (a) you want a doctoral degree simply for your own satisfaction or (b) you are seeking further education that may open future doors, be certain you choose a field and a topic for research that you really love. You will be spending the next 3 to 6 years totally immersed in the field and specifically engaged in an area in which you will become an expert. If you don't find your study fascinating and enthralling, you will likely not finish. Even those of us who absolutely love what we are researching will be sick of the study at some point.

FIND THE RIGHT PROGRAM

Beyond the basic question of which field of study you should pursue, there are additional questions for you to consider, such as the manner in which the degree is offered and whether or not there are expectations for students to commit to full-time study. For those primarily interested in traditional fields of research (such as science, engineering, or arts and letters) and who want to enter into academia, you may be expected to be a full-time, traditional student and perhaps engaged at the university as a graduate assistant. For others, especially those in professional degree areas such as education, health services, or business, there may be other choices.

Many universities have developed program delivery options for working professionals that may include online courses or weekend seminars. Although these delivery options provide some flexibility and choice for students, you should carefully investigate their rigor and expectations. Many reputable state and private universities offer such options and expect students to do the same high-quality work as if they were full-time students. In many ways, these programs can be more difficult, as you will be working full time as well as taking coursework and conducting your dissertation research. Be prepared for this.

Some programs may offer a less rigorous degree or one that minimizes research preparation. Be cautious. While you may be tempted to pursue a degree program that sounds like less work, is this what you really want? Investigate the reputation of the program and whether or not it will provide you the credentials you need and want to pursue your goals.

CHOOSE YOUR DISSERTATION CHAIR WISELY

Once you have found the program that is right for you, you should know that the most important person in your life for the next few years will be your dissertation chair. To the extent possible, take an active role in choosing your chair. Some programs give you complete choice, or you may even discuss this with the faculty member you wish to work with prior to applying for the program.

Other programs may allow you some input but make the final decision as to who is assigned as your chair. Even if you don't have full choice, be certain that you contribute relevant information regarding your interests and learning style in order to help program faculty make better decisions about which faculty members would be the best matches for you.

In choosing a chair, first and foremost, consider your area of interest and specialty. Your chair should have the necessary knowledge and expertise to guide you in your study. Second, consider your learning style and the faculty member's teaching style. Are they compatible? For instance, if you are someone who likes to work under deadlines and needs orderly direction, you will probably be most successful with a chair that will provide these for you or respond to your deadlines.

Do you need someone who will gently push you or someone who leaves it up to you to make appointments and meet deadlines? Finally, consider your comfort level with the faculty member. This will be someone you must work with closely at every stage of your research. It is important that you feel comfortable asking the faculty member questions, seeking his or her advice, accepting critique, and engaging in intellectual dialogue about your topic.

You should trust that your chair wants you to be successful. From my perspective, there is nothing more rewarding than the one-to-one mentoring relationship between chair and student. Doctoral level work is like nothing you've experienced before. Although technically a student, you are in actuality working as a colleague with your chair. The chair-student/colleague relationship will likely continue over a lifetime, either through continued mutual research and writing or through professional networking.

WORK STRATEGICALLY

One purpose of a doctoral program is to expand one's horizons and open one's thinking to new ideas. Although exciting, information overload can create some potential roadblocks for doctoral students. Sometimes students become energized by each new course and constantly change the direction of their dissertation study. These students often end up as 6- or 8-year completers, or worse, ABD (All But Dissertation). On the other hand, focusing on a study too early (before appropriate coursework) and stubbornly refusing to budge from this line of inquiry may result in an early graduation but a less than desirable topic or dissertation. Find a happy medium.

Many times students begin a program with some idea of where they want to focus their doctoral dissertation research. Even if a "problem of study" is fuzzy or ill-defined, you should begin exploring the research surrounding this topic as soon as you begin the program. When possible, choose topics for papers or literature reviews assigned in your coursework that will help you learn more about your future dissertation research.

Begin to work with your chair and other faculty on an individual basis, seeking their advice about the topic and perhaps doing independent studies that provide credit for your work. These strategies will help you define your study. Finding that a particular topic really does not hold your interest is as valuable as finding one that does. The sooner you begin to explore in depth the questions you think you want to pursue in a dissertation, the sooner you can seriously start the study itself.

Some programs, by design, will provide more consistent support for research and writing than others. Regardless of the amount of support built into the program, finishing the work of dissertation research is up to you. Commit to a multiyear program of study and stay focused. Early in your coursework develop a routine for regular study and writing. There is no time or routine better than another—only one that works for you.

Consider your commitments to work, family, and other activities and carve out time that is reserved solely for your doctoral study and dissertation research. Make this a firm schedule. Think of it in the same way as you would think about going to work each day. It is not negotiable. For some, the most productive time may be midnight to 2 A.M. each day; for others the best time is 5 to 7 A.M.; and yet, others will devote every Saturday from 8 A.M. to 5 P.M.

Finally, don't make yourself crazy. Rely on your support system of other doctoral students, friends, and families. Take appropriate vacations and mental health breaks. Continue to take care of yourself and enjoy one of the most rewarding experiences of your life.

4

Life in the Fast Lane: Beginning the Doctoral Process

Dr. Page A. Smith
University of Texas–San Antonio

Much exists in the literature about beginning a program of doctoral studies. In fact, a considerable portion of this literature presents what I believe are "hard-wired" templates designed to enable doctoral beginners to establish effective normative patterns that will lead to early programmatic successes. My contribution deals specifically with what I believe is a common anxiety affecting neophyte doctoral students; namely, the hesitancy to act after being accepted into the program. What follows is an early pep talk that I often use to encourage my students.

Let's be frank, it's not uncommon for a newly admitted doctoral student to experience anxiety paralysis during the onset of his or her program. However, you've already accomplished so much by addressing the realities of the admissions process, the Graduate Record Examination (GRE), and a series of application interviews and procedures. In fact, you may feel you've all but exhausted your reserve of talent and that your motivational tank is empty!

Don't worry; it's perfectly natural to feel a bit "out of orbit" about pursuing your doctorate. Instead of fretting about what to do and how to do it, maybe you should just get started. In doctoral studies, like many other areas of life, the beginning often determines the end. So let's take a moment and reframe the issue of your doctoral studies program by examining some reasons students use for not starting. Then, we'll unpack the good stuff about you and your program!

One of the most common reasons for not starting is perfection; and doctoral students are particularly prone to perfectionism. Although striving for perfection is an admirable trait, it often parallelizes doctoral students. I suggest diving right in and through persistence and the help of a capable doctoral committee, your scholarship will blossom. No doubt about it! In essence, beginning your doctoral journey is a lot like steering an elephant. You can climb aboard the elephant (your program) and wait for it to move, or you can instigate movement and influence the direction and speed of your doctoral studies.

Another reason for not initiating action is cloaked in the thinking that leads students to apply to doctoral programs. In interview situations, I often hear a student claim, "Getting my doctorate has always been my dream." The problem is when a student is admitted to a program, he or she sometimes continues to dream about tomorrow instead of acting today.

Ultimately, this well-intentioned line of thinking produces stagnated progression and faulty starts. So let's agree to concentrate on today's tasks and let tomorrow's concerns rest. Remember that you were selected into your program because others realized your potential. By targeting important day-to-day tasks and developing a routine of taking care of today's business, you simply reinforce what others already believe.

It is important to understand that the doctoral selection committee saw something special about you. They saw something unique about you and your potential that sets you apart from all others. The faith the committee vested in you by virtue of your acceptance into the program reaffirms my belief that you can seize the moment and press on without prompting.

As a result of your acceptance into your program, motivation is replaced by momentum and your upcoming curriculum is simply an extension of your progress. Channel your momentum into productive areas that result in your success. At this point, momentum is more valuable than motivation.

There's an old cliché about thinking big, but starting small. When you begin, don't plan on understanding what it takes to get to the mountaintop, just take the next step. Devise processes for small wins, master the details under your control by playing to your strengths, connect deeply but not abruptly with your advisor, seek counsel from past and present doctoral students, and plan to achieve victory after victory by daily meeting realistic goals that have been preestablished.

It's important to categorize the steps and functions that lead to your initial victories. In doing so, you'll further fuel your momentum by developing what works into habits, thus increasing the speed at which you can navigate future tasks. This is true for deciding what priorities and skills are needed for a particular project. By prioritizing the steps necessary for completing the job and determining the immediate tasks, you control the situation.

In conclusion, starting the process begins with you. I have no question that you possess the stamina necessary to excel! I've often heard the expression that will power is directly proportionate to want power. If you want it bad enough, you'll muster the will to achieve it. Recognize your current progress (but never rest on it), keep the momentum going, and remember it's always easier to move from minor setbacks to success than it is from excuses to success. Where does all this talk lead? It leads to you—controlling your destiny. You're on your way to a great experience!

5

Beginning the Doctoral Journey

Dr. Pamela A. Angelle
The University of Tennessee

You have decided to pursue the doctorate. Achieving this goal will place you in an elite group and make you an expert in your field of study. At the end of your journey, you will receive the terminal degree, and you will be recognized as a scholar and researcher. You are beginning an adventure that will be filled with joy and excitement, frustration and fear. So now that you have made your reservations for this journey, as someone who has previously walked this road, I offer a few points to keep in mind as you travel.

PLAN YOUR TRIP

The trip is easier if you know where you are going. Knowledge and understanding of your course requirements are an important first step. If possible, find out from the department chairperson if a master schedule has been generated. Be cognizant of the balance of coursework. Before you schedule your courses each semester, consider the rigor of the coursework, your foundational knowledge, and your experience with specific issues in the course content.

Understand the parameters of electives according to your program. Can you take any elective classes? Or, must the class be offered outside of the program or department; be a research class or pertain to your dissertation topic; or, be approved by your advisor? Knowing the answers to these questions will help you while planning coursework.

Another critical point is to understand program residency requirements. Knowing program expectations will help you plan the appropriate time to complete the residency, particularly if you are working full time to pursue your degree. Will you be required to be a full-time student with no outside employment, or, can you schedule 9 hours of coursework each semester for a year as you continue with your career?

The doctoral degree can be achieved through careful planning. Looking ahead with the end in mind will make the smoother journey. It is important to understand the pivotal points of the program of study along the road.

UNDERSTAND THE TERRAIN

As you travel the road to your degree, knowing the requirements is important. Equally important is an understanding of what the requirements mean. One requirement is comprehensive exams. Preparing for comprehensive exams begins when you walk into your first class; therefore, understand the examination and defense processes in your program or department. Another requirement is the dissertation. What are the components of a dissertation? How do you go about deciding on a topic and area of interest?

The map of the doctoral terrain is filled with unfamiliar terms to those outside academe. Terms such as dissertation, residency, APA (American Psychological Association), IRB (institutional review board), comprehensive exams, "the literature," "the field," "the findings" will become second nature as you move along your journey. You will begin to understand the terrain through your coursework. Some programs offer seminars in dissertation writing and beginning the literature review. Taking advantage of these opportunities will lighten your anxiety. Finding a travel guide can be particularly helpful in negotiating the doctoral terrain.

FIND A TRAVEL GUIDE

As with any journey, connect with someone who has experienced this journey. He or she knows the terrain and knows what lies ahead. This will make the trip smoother for you. At times, the journey is stressful.

You want a travel guide who is patient and available because you will have many questions. Choose a guide who can help you negotiate your roadblocks and detours and support you in moments of anxiety—cheering your accomplishments and assuaging your fears.

While encouragement is important, a guide who holds you accountable at those times when you experience jet lag is critical. Evening classes, intense reading, writing assignments, and the general rigor of coursework can be taxing. Having someone to "hold your feet to the fire" will keep you motivated and on the right path.

Find a guide with similar interests as you. If you are interested in the principalship, policy, or instructional strategies, finding a likeminded mentor will increase your likelihood of success. Advice from someone who is an expert in your area will ensure that bumps in the road are lessened. Your guide should provide honest feedback with the goal of improvement. This is all part of the process, so develop a thick skin and accept feedback as part of your learning. Of course, when you hit those bumps in the road, it is always comforting to turn to colleagues who are negotiating the same ruts and potholes.

TRAVEL IN GROUPS

Although there will be times when you travel alone, on long journeys it is best to travel in groups. Touring unfamiliar places with others ensures a network of support, information, and commiseration. Though not everyone who begins the journey with you will be there in the end, having traveling companions along the way can help.

Setting up study groups to prepare for exams and coursework allows you to talk through subject matter. Hearing someone else's view on course material may clarify and strengthen your thinking. When there is a large volume of information, such as preparing for comprehensive exams, colleagues can help you to "divide and conquer."

Writing groups are invaluable as you travel through your coursework. A writing partner can read your work, and vice versa, offering feedback on your content and writing style. Critical friends who move through the program alongside you can be vital to surviving the intense reading and writing workload.

Equally important is the emotional support from others who take this journey. Mutual commiseration and empathy are essential at those times when you begin to feel overwhelmed. Times of accomplishment and success are best celebrated with those who recognize the toil that went into the task.

If you are in a cohort model program, you begin with "built-in" travel companions. Through the cohort model, small groups of students journey through coursework together, often with the same advisor. However, if the program you are enrolled in does not offer a cohort program, no need to worry. In those first courses, everyone is a stranger; however, strangers quickly become friends.

COLLECT SOUVENIRS ALONG THE WAY

As you make your way along this road, the topic of your dissertation will take shape. Small nuggets of information begin to churn, forming larger questions as possibilities for research. I call these "souvenirs" from courses and encounters with professors. At the beginning, these mementos are small, but they will increase in value over time. Collect and file them. Initially, the souvenirs may be unformed notes or random thoughts; however, as you progress through your program and increase your knowledge of the research literature, they will form into an area of thought, perhaps becoming a question to answer in your dissertation.

As you learn theory and course material, you must learn to ponder. Spend some time in rumination, considering your souvenirs and reflecting on what you read, what you hear from your professors, and what you know from your experiences. As a doctoral student, it will be important for you to become an avid reader, a proficient and prolific writer, but equally important, is to become a thinker.

KEEP YOUR TRAVEL COSTS REASONABLE

Even the best intention to maintain balance in your work, school, or home is challenging. Time with family becomes time at home with books. Fast food becomes common because time is spent reading journal articles and writing another paper. Physical movement becomes a thing of the past because sitting in front of the computer is how you spend your time. Along the way, keep the travel costs reasonable. Set goals for your coursework and your dissertation, but don't forget to set goals for your life. Take time for your family. Take time for you. Completing the doctoral program is possible if you are mentally, emotionally, and physically prepared.

A FINAL TRAVEL TIP

Congratulations on taking the first step in the journey of a lifetime! There will be days when you think this trip will never end. Then, all of a sudden, you have reached your destination. You are standing in front of friends and family. Your major professor is placing a colorful and symbolic hood on your shoulders. The trip will be long, at times arduous, but always worth the price of the ticket. So, as you embark on this journey, my final travel tip is to enjoy the ride.

6

Considerations at the Threshold: The Beginning of Doctoral Studies

Dr. María Luisa González
University of Texas–El Paso

After 21 years in the academy and a long list of doctoral graduates, I have concluded that each student is a unique individual and is affected by different sociocultural factors such as educational experiences, race, ethnicity, physical challenges, and gender. In the context of these factors, one thing is certain—most students enter doctoral programs with the necessary skills to obtain their doctoral degrees. However, some students encounter obstacles associated with obtaining their doctorate. So let's take a realistic look at some things that affect the beginning of what I believe is going to be a wonderfully productive venture for you.

Sometimes students forget they are free to make choices. They complete the application process and are admitted to a doctoral program. With acceptance into the program, they accept decision-making responsibilities. Take control of your choices at the onset of the doctoral program.

Remember that a doctoral degree represents the pinnacle of academic success and is completely different from a master's degree in both quality and rigor. The master's degree is largely about coursework; the doctorate involves completing a dissertation. It's generally not the coursework involved with doctoral studies that poses the greatest challenge to success. It's writing a quality dissertation that poses the challenge. Set your sights on doing both a first-rate job in class and producing a quality dissertation near the end of your program—and you won't go wrong!

Another challenge germane to the doctoral process is maintaining the proper balance between your life as a doctoral student and your life in general. Maintaining the proper balance to your life is important! To respond to the demands of doctoral studies, take care of your physical, mental, and emotional health. Maintain wellness by healthy eating, regular exercise, and scheduling time for family, studies, and friends. When multitasking, things can become stressful. So, establish a healthy and workable game plan for success at the onset of your doctoral undertaking. That way, you begin with the odds stacked in your favor.

Another important facet of a successful doctoral experience is to identify why you're pursuing the degree. In most professors' experiences (including my own), personal determinants play a major role in developing the perseverance needed for success. Ask the question "Why do I truly want a doctorate?" The doctorate, for example, may lead to advancement or a higher paying salary. Still others may have a master's degree and feel the next logical step is to work on a doctorate, or that becoming a scholar is important. Your motivation for pursuing the doctorate represents an important beginning to the doctoral process.

In fact, your motivation in pursuing a doctoral degree may help determine the type of degree or program you pursue. Oftentimes, for students involved in education programs, the major decision is choosing between the Ph.D. or the Ed.D. My advice is to investigate the differences between the two options, make a rational decision, and commence the journey.

Another factor to consider when beginning a doctoral program is whether to join a cohort-based program or one where individual studies are the norm. Many programs don't offer options between the two models; therefore, it's important to preselect your preferred model before applying. Preplanning and reflection at the start of your program will prove to be incredibly beneficial to you.

Determine whether you are going to work while pursuing your doctoral studies. As a full-time employee and a part-time doctoral student, challenges escalate. When working full time there are many issues to handle such as balancing the personal, professional, and academic components of your life. Conversely, full-time graduate students experience different pressures but have more opportunities to work directly with faculty in a research-based environment.

I realize the dissertation seems in the distant future to you; however, I believe it is helpful to present a few thoughts about the end of your journey at the beginning of your program. Almost all universities require a dissertation to earn a doctorate, and to successfully complete one, students need to be adept at writing. Your ability to write well will be a major factor in obtaining your doctorate.

As you begin your trek toward doctoral success, access and read dissertations of interest to get a taste of what's ahead. Consider subscribing to research-oriented journals in your field to deepen your knowledge base. Supplemental reading, in addition to those required in your studies, is critical to success. Ask professors to give you a list of dissertations and seminal works they feel are outstanding. These readings will assist you in assimilating to the rigor of writing required of you.

My final piece of advice involves the selection of your doctoral chair. From personal experience, I see many students ask the most "popular" professor to chair their work. Select a chair or advisor who is an expert in your area of study. I recommend going with expertise first and then determine if you can work closely with that individual according to personality and fit. Invariably your decision involves the process of selecting potential chairs and then progressing through the process of elimination. Ultimately, it is crucial to work with a chair who is interested in your research topic and who respects you as a student. The process ultimately begins and ends with you. To achieve what you're striving for, embrace the major investments in the time, planning, and commitment necessary to reach the doctoral "dream" and get moving!

7

Just Beginning a Doctoral Program?

Dr. CarolAnne M. Kardash
University of Nevada, Las Vegas

Dr. Jeanne T. Amlund
The Pennsylvania State University, Greater Allegheny

So you have been admitted to the doctoral program. Let's chat a bit about how you can get off to a good start. Before you begin your first semester, take time to read the research being published by the professors in your department. Don't limit your reading to the work of professors you may have been thinking about working with when you applied to the doctoral program. Explore the areas of interest for every professor and make note of those who involve doctoral students in their research projects.

Take advantage of every opportunity to participate in formal and informal gatherings with professors to discuss research as well as any opportunities offered to participate in ongoing research projects. It doesn't matter whether or not the professors' research projects match your initial research interests. Your goal at the beginning of your program should be to learn as much as you can about conducting research. The research methodology and statistical analysis skills you will begin to acquire by being part of a research team are generic, so these skills will transfer to the research questions you are interested in investigating. The more research you do, the easier it becomes.

Moreover, getting to know your professors early on by working with them on their research projects will be useful later when you need to select a dissertation advisor and committee members. And, learning about the research interests and areas of expertise of all the professors in your department may help you to better define and refine your own research interests.

As you begin your first semester, get to know other doctoral students in the program. Other doctoral students are able to provide invaluable "insider" information about navigating the pitfalls and required hurdles necessary to progress through the doctoral program successfully. These doctoral students provide vital information that you might not be able to get from other sources. You need to make yourself available to work on research that is being conducted by your fellow doctoral students. These students are your future professional colleagues and collaborators. The more involved you can be in collaborating with other students in designing research studies, assisting in preparing research materials, and collecting and collating data, the better your preparation to conduct your own research.

When working with others on research projects, keep in mind that not all contributions to a research study merit authorship. Before you commit to participate on a research study, clarify with your colleagues whether the tasks you are slated to perform will merit authorship and, if so, where in the order of authorship your contribution will be positioned.

This information will help to prevent hurt feelings or to compromise future professional relationships. Keep in mind as well that it takes a long time before a study gets published—sometimes as much as 1 to 2 years after a manuscript has been submitted initially for possible publication in a journal. Thus, it's in your best interest to get involved in research projects as soon as possible.

Another good way to get to know doctoral students in your program is to participate in graduate student organizations, sponsored research-related activities, and regularly scheduled graduate student research presentations at your university. Be open to getting acquainted with doctoral students and faculty in your same discipline at other institutions. You can do this by joining listservs devoted to research topics in which you are interested and by attending graduate seminars at national conferences sponsored by professional organizations such as the American Educational Research Association.

The importance of working with others in your discipline throughout your doctoral program cannot be overemphasized. Begin your studies with an open mind, determined to broaden and deepen your knowledge. Identify, think about, and discuss with others the important questions being asked and answered through research in your field. Take the time to consider how any preconceived research questions you might have had in mind for your own research when you entered the program fit into the larger picture of your discipline. Once well informed about the current research directions in your field, you will narrow your perspective to target a specific question as the focus for your doctoral research.

At this point in your education, you should be well aware of your academic strengths and weaknesses. If your weaknesses will impact your ability to complete the requirements of the doctoral program, or limit your subsequent success as a competent academic professional, it will be up to you to address these weaknesses. For example, completing additional statistics or advanced writing for publication courses may be necessary to fill the gaps in your background. Plan to complete the requirements of your doctoral program as soon as possible; however, do not pass up opportunities to take coursework that is not required with "visiting" and accomplished scholars in your field.

Take your required research methodology and statistics courses as early as possible in your program. Take as many classes in both quantitative and qualitative research methods as possible. Being at ease with both of these research approaches is the single best way to broaden the research questions you are able to ask. Expertise in research methodology and statistical analyses not only increases the likelihood that professors and other doctoral students will want to include you in their research projects, but also it will enhance your marketability considerably when the time comes for you to seek a professional position.

Seek out challenging classes and professors. Avail yourself of the opportunity to get to know these professors on a more personal level by visiting them during their office hours. Keep in mind that rigorous classes can equate to deeper learning. That added learning will bring dividends later in your doctoral program as you develop and defend your dissertation as well as participate in other research studies.

Use each class to inform your research agenda. Developing research questions from insights gained in class or designing a study based on an ANOVA (analysis of variance) statistical procedure are examples of using your classes to inform your research. Similarly, if you are personally interested in self-efficacy and enrolled in a seminar on learning strategies, you might design a study to investigate how self-efficacy influences the strategies learners use.

Decide now, before you begin, how you are going to keep track of your readings. Set up a system for filing hard and electronic copies of articles, book chapters, and other documents. You will be reading thousands of pages during your first semester. Avoid wasting hours later in the program searching for a needed document you read earlier in the program.

Consider purchasing binders for each of your classes as a way to collect, file, and locate class information. You can refer to "binder" information as you progress through your doctoral program. Binders containing information from your classes may also prove invaluable if you later obtain an academic position where you are asked to teach similar classes.

You will need to keep a record of everything you read including a citation to retrieve the document, location of your hard or electronic copy, if available, along with a brief summary of points you found to be relevant or interesting. Transcribing handwritten notes or index cards into a database on your computer will make searching for specific items more efficient as well as serve as a backup of your handwritten records. Handwritten documents get lost, electronic files get deleted by mistake, and hard drives crash. You will want to protect yourself from what can be a devastating loss of your records and work by learning to backup records you maintain on your computer on a regular basis and finding a means to store your backups securely online or offsite.

Along with your reading, you should spend time thinking about what you read and discussing with others what you think about what you have read. As part of this process, consider reflective journaling to keep a record of your thoughts and ideas. Try to come up with several new ideas to record in your journal each day.

Start building your curriculum vita as soon as possible. Early involvement in research studies will contribute to the "research and scholarship" portion of your vita. Opportunities that you may have in your doctoral program to serve as a graduate assistant or primary instructor for sections of undergraduate and master's levels classes will contribute to the "teaching experience" portion of your vita. Start to build the "service" portion of your vita by volunteering to review conference proposals and manuscripts for possible publication for journals in your field. Be sure to ask your advisor as well as other faculty members about such opportunities.

Finally, avoid allowing the demands of your doctoral program to become so all consuming that you lose sight of your family and personal life. Learning to maintain a healthy and professionally productive balance between your professional and personal life will be important not only during your doctoral studies but throughout your academic career.

AUTHORS' NOTE

We wish to thank Ordene Edwards, a doctoral student in the Department of Educational Psychology at the University of Nevada, Las Vegas, for her comments on an earlier version of this manuscript.

8

You're Sure You Really Want to Do This?

Dr. Stephen Jacobson
University at Buffalo–State University of New York

Okay, it's time to set the record straight. I know you really think you *want* to get a doctorate, but I want to be sure that you really know exactly what you're getting yourself into now that you've been accepted into doctoral studies. First, earning a doctorate is *not* to be confused with completing another, only lengthier, master's program. And a dissertation is *not* to be confused with completing another, only lengthier, final project. Granted, the initial coursework will seem familiar, and if you were an "A" student in your master's studies, which is probably the case, then chances are good that you'll probably ace most of your first-year doctoral courses.

Now you must keep in mind that your coursework is simply a means to an end and that these classes are intended to provide the foundation for the real work that lies ahead. Getting "A"s in your courses will be all well and good, but developing a researchable question, designing an appropriate methodology for the question(s) you pose, collecting and appropriately analyzing your data, and then offering sensible conclusions and recommendations based on your findings are what really matter in the end.

You may be surprised to learn that we don't grade dissertations. Just ask around, no one gets an A, A–, B+, or any other grade on their thesis; you either successfully complete the project or you don't. And unlike most course assignments, which are essentially over the minute you hand it in, your thesis isn't done until your committee says it's done. So be prepared to work and rework and perhaps once again rework a sentence, paragraph, section, or chapter. Don't get "wed" to your words, because a "divorce" is imminent. This is the life you've chosen. Somewhere in the future, you'll look back and realize that your coursework was the easiest, most socially engaging part of your doctoral experience.

The starting and end dates, as well as the class hours, of your courses are clear. The instructor most likely identified all of your class readings in advance on the course syllabus and the required assignments and assessments, as I already noted, will typically be "one bite of the apple" experiences that yield a grade, and voila, you're done. In some instances you may be assigned group projects in which the workload and the insights drawn from the project can be shared.

This is learning with a social component, sometimes resulting in positive experiences, sometimes not, but as much as you may at times feel overwhelmed by the coursework, enjoy the experience and draw as much as you can from it while it lasts because the next phase of the adventure is different.

This second phase, when you're called a doctoral candidate, is the point where you begin to venture into the realm of independent researcher. I trust you'll be successful with your comprehensive exam or qualifying paper because it is really just a summative assessment of your coursework, but the conceptualizing required for the dissertation proposal is where the road gets steep. In fact, this is most often when some folks earn their ABD (All But Dissertation) and opt to leave the program.

Now the work starts to get lonely, there are no more courses as it's just you and your advisor(s) as you search to find your unique place in the field relative to the literature you've reviewed. As you work through the proposal and subsequently the collection and analysis of your data, you may start to obsess about your topic. As a result, people may seem like they're trying to avoid you as your conversation becomes increasingly narrow, focused almost exclusively on your work and your study.

Chances are they *are* trying to avoid you, so better have a good support network in place and be kind and understanding to family and friends, because chances are that you *are* becoming as boring as they think you are. You may even start to dream about your data!! This is when you've hit the low point—Dissertation Valley. It's not as hot as Death Valley, but it feels pretty desolate. You'll wonder why you ever got yourself into this mess and start to feel as if life, your life, is slipping away under a pile of surveys, interview transcripts, or SPSS (Statistical Package for the Social Sciences) data runs.

Hang in there. If you really have some fire in your belly about your study, you'll soon start to climb out of the valley. The questions you've posed are questions that need answers and if not now, when? And, if not by you, then who? Yes, this is important work; this study can make a contribution! You'll find your energy and enthusiasm renewed and, finally, that fateful day will arrive, the public defense of your dissertation findings. There in the room will be your committee members. They may have been helpful, they may have driven you nuts, but collectively they possessed the expertise you needed to complete the project.

You will suddenly realize that what you have been doing the past few years has been an apprenticeship in one of the world's oldest guilds, and that these master scholars in front of you will now determine whether you can be a member of their craft. And then, if all goes well in the defense, you'll feel like you are engaged in conversation among peers. You'll realize that you are actually quite knowledgeable about the topic you've researched, perhaps the best versed about that specific issue of any in the room. And after about an hour or so, the committee will ask you to step outside the room while they deliberate your fate, and when the door finally reopens, you will be greeted with, "Congratulations, Doctor!"

After the initial euphoria wears off, there comes a sense of loss. You have kept your eye on the prize and achieved your goal. Now you realize that this stage of your life is over and, that over the course of whatever number of years it takes, you will be a different person. So what should you take from all of this? It's simple; today you are beginning an exciting journey. Never lose sight of your objectives, but try hard to appreciate the experience as you are in the midst of achieving them, because you'll never go down road this again. Now, don't you have some books to buy and some reading to do?

II

CONQUERING COMMON DOCTORAL CHALLENGES: MOTIVATION, PROCRASTINATION, AND REENERGIZING

This section of *The Doctoral Student's Advisor and Mentor* is dedicated to the structure of the dissertation for doctoral studies. The mentoring advice offered by these exceptional faculty addresses low motivation, ABD (All But Dissertation), finding your passion, and reenergizing doctoral students.

- Dr. Bruce W. Tuckman: Getting Over the "ABD" Hump: The Secret Is Avoiding Procrastination
- Dr. Stacey Edmonson: Avoid Being Labeled ABD
- Dr. Connie L. Fulmer: When Motivation Hits Bottom
- Dr. Megan Tschannen-Moran: Passion: Don't Embark Without It
- Dr. Patrick D. Pauken: Brains, Heart, Courage, and Home: When Doctoral Students Have Significant Personal Issues Confounding the Completion of the Dissertation

9

Getting Over the "ABD" Hump: The Secret Is Avoiding Procrastination

Dr. Bruce W. Tuckman
The Ohio State University

Procrastination is the "thief of time." It's time spent without getting anything in return. When you are a graduate student, time is precious; you must use it as fully as you can. But often that is not what happens. Instead, when faced with a challenge of great magnitude, a dissertation for example, you have a tendency to use rationalizations to provide yourself with reasons for not getting started. "I don't really know how to do it!" "I just can't seem to get started." "I'm just waiting for the best time to do it." "I need to be in the mood." "No one really cares if I do this or not."

But these are not the real reasons why you procrastinate. You have hidden the real reasons from yourself to protect your ego. So what are the real reasons? At the top of the list is lack of self-confidence; you don't believe that you can write a dissertation. It's too big a job; you don't know where to start; you don't know what problem to study; you don't know what's expected of you, and you're afraid to find out. You are looking for a simple problem to study and you can't find one. You don't believe you can do it. Most people don't take on any challenge they believe they can't meet. They are licked before they start.

Another reason is perfectionism. The more you try working on a dissertation, the more you believe it will not be good enough. You are using this reasoning as an excuse for not getting started or for stopping midstream. Feeling overwhelmed by the magnitude of the task is likely to lead to depression. And if you are looking for immediate gratification, you're not likely to start working on something that's going to take a long time to finish.

Carrie felt like an old car without any gas. She just could not seem to get herself started. Maybe she was sick. She had not felt good ever since she completed her candidacy exam and began to think about a dissertation topic. She knew that she needed to get started on her dissertation, but she just did not seem to have the energy. Perhaps if she took a little rest, she could work on the dissertation tomorrow.

On her way to the couch, she suddenly stopped. This was the kind of rationalizing she had heard about in her educational psychology class. This was not the kind of person she wanted to be. So she started a different conversation with herself. Actually, it was more of a lecture.

"You're smart, you're healthy, you can do this dissertation. So get off your butt and get started!"

Carrie was shocked. She sounded like her grandmother. This was enough to put some fuel in her tank. She felt more in charge and she even had some energy. It seemed as if the rationalization had drained her. Getting positive and telling herself the truth charged her up (adapted from Tuckman, Abry, & Smith, 2008, p. 35).

What ABD students need to deal with is the procrastination cycle. It starts out with your finding yourself in a potentially difficult situation, namely having to write a dissertation (or suffer the consequences of having an ABD rather than a Ph.D.). The perceived difficulty of the situation triggers a thought or belief about yourself: "I can't do it." This thought leads to a feeling: anxiety, fear, or anger, or some combination of the three, making you feel squeezed, which, in turn, leads to a behavior: avoidance, procrastination. And so it goes; no dissertation!

Now you can see what is going on inside you. You've become aware of why you're on the ABD track. That's a big first step! Now you have to take the second step: How to get yourself going. How to overcome procrastination. Here are my time-tested recommendations:

1. Start keeping track of how you spend your time, a prerequisite for time management. Make a table of the hours in a day and write down what you did each hour. Use this table to help you identify the conditions under which you accomplished the most work on your dissertation. Ask yourself how you could rearrange your schedule to

get more work done on your dissertation. Make sure you insert short breaks in your work schedule so you don't burn out, but then return to your work after each break.
2. Your work schedule should be made up of what I call "bite-sized pieces." Start out small; don't try to do too much at one time. "Don't bite off more than you can chew." It can have negative consequences on your progress.
3. Set short-term goals for what you want to accomplish. Make the goals challenging but attainable. The goals should apply to the progress of your dissertation. You can set daily or weekly benchmarks to help keep yourself on task.
4. Now here is the recommendation with the most oomph! Build a weekly work plan. I call it a to-do checklist. At the beginning of each week, make a chart with each day of the week on it. For each day, list what work you will do on your dissertation. Don't just write: "I will work on my dissertation." That is not specific enough to be helpful. Right down exactly what you will do (for example: "I will write my hypotheses;" "I will go to the library and search for references on my main topic"; "I will meet with my advisor"; "I will write down ideas for my methodology"). Then look at each day on your checklist and check it off when you have completed it. This will keep you on task.
5. Choose a topic that you are comfortable with, interested in, and practical (i.e., workable), from a methodological point of view. Remember, you're not necessarily out for a dissertation award, you're out for a doctorate. Look through journals that relate to your interests and find some good ideas for your own work. Read other people's dissertations to provide you with models for your own. Try to build up your self-confidence by seeing what others have done.
6. Don't burn yourself out trying to write the whole dissertation at once. Write a 10-page prospectus describing your research topic, hypotheses, and methodology. It's a good "warm-up" activity for your dissertation. Ask your advisor to read it and to give you feedback.
7. Be kind to yourself! Give yourself rewards after you complete some part of your dissertation. Write personal affirmations (e.g., "I'm good at this research stuff!") and stick them on your refrigerator.

Don't depend on your advisor to push you, but keep in close touch with him or her.
8. Don't let yourself lose momentum after you finish each section of your dissertation. Maintain a steady pace! It's like running a marathon, but your legs don't get as sore.

If you can find a copy of my textbook *Conducting Educational Research* (5th ed.) in your library (it's gone out of print, but it will still be in libraries), look at chapter 12—"Writing a Research Report"— and chapter 15—"Analyzing and Critiquing a Research Study." These will be of great help as you write your dissertation.

REFERENCES

Tuckman, B. W. (1999). *Conducting educational research* (5th ed.). Fort Worth, TX: Harcourt Brace.

Tuckman, B. W., Abry, D. A., & Smith, D. R. (2008). *Learning and motivation strategies: Your guide to success* (2nd ed.). Upper Saddle River, NJ: Pearson/Prentice Hall.

10

Avoid Being Labeled ABD

Dr. Stacey Edmonson
Sam Houston State University

Thomas Alva Edison noted that "Success is 10 percent inspiration and 90 percent perspiration." He may not have been a doctoral student at the time, but Edison definitely knew how to describe the dissertation process! If the dissertation were easy, everyone would have a terminal degree.

What separates students who have "Dr." in front of their names from those who don't is often completing the dissertation. Let's be honest— generally, most students accepted into a doctoral program can complete the coursework, but an unfortunate number fail to complete the dissertation successfully. Why? I think students stall at completing the dissertation for reasons other than intelligence or capacity. Frankly, many students founder at the dissertation stage because they lack the motivation to push beyond their coursework.

Throughout the first several years of your doctoral program, you were given a specific set of externally imposed guidelines that helped keep you on track. Your program director told you what courses to take and probably even told you in what order to take them.

For every course you had a syllabus with specific due dates for each assignment. It's likely you were given specific guidelines regarding what each assignment was to entail—things such as the type of content required, the purpose of the assignment, and possibly prescriptions regarding a project's length and style.

The consequences of performing or not performing were explicit and often immediate in the form of grades and evaluations. But now, at the dissertation stage, there is no one imposing external guidelines on you. It's all on your shoulders. If the due dates and specific guidelines found in your coursework were critical tools for your success, replicate them for yourself during the dissertation process.

The external forces that were in place to ensure your success in the doctoral program have been removed, and now you have to find the impetus for success internally. Hence, the first step in dealing with this shift from an external locus of control to an internal one is to recognize the importance of this change and its impact on you throughout the dissertation process. Once you recognize that the structures for completing the dissertation are self-developed and self-regulated, you can then remind yourself that yes, you can do this and yes, you will navigate successfully through the dissertation.

One trap you want to avoid as you begin the dissertation is the perception that you now have an abundance of new or extra time because you no longer have organized classes. Students often underestimate the impact that the absence of classes has on their abilities to respond to the demands of self-directed productivity. They tend to think, "I'm a committed student, I want to finish the program—this won't be a problem." However, they fail to adjust to the priority shift that takes place when the external dictates that kept you on track in your coursework are removed.

Let me illustrate this with an example. Before starting the doctoral program, it was likely you had a full-time job and a busy family or personal life. Subsequently, you added doctoral coursework to a schedule that was already busy and full. Somehow you made it all work—a true testimony to your abilities!

Beware—after you've finished with coursework, things such as the full-time job, your personal life, and other obligations will quickly surface to fill in the "spare time" you feel you now have in the absence of organized coursework. In order to avoid this trap, I strongly encourage you to maintain your routine as though you are still involved in coursework. In fact, I believe you will be well served to set aside as many hours to work on your dissertation as you did to prepare for your coursework. That way, your work routine stays the same and only the focus of your efforts is redirected. This can be hard to do, which is why you need to make it a priority. You might even need to drive to campus and sit in the library in order to really make this happen. It can be tempting to start enjoying or committing time to those things that you sacrificed during your years of coursework, but it's not time to relax quite yet!

Treating the composition of your dissertation with the same energy you dedicated to your coursework will allow you to make your document a priority and prevent you from falling back into the "busy-ness" you knew before entering the doctoral program. If you can remain disciplined with a specific work regimen for the dissertation, just like you did with your courses, you will find the dissertation to be a "doable" project.

Another motivating factor to consider when advancing to the dissertation-writing phase is the investment you made by joining a doctoral program. For several years, you dedicated yourself, your time, energy, and money to achieving the goal of becoming "Dr." No one starts a doctoral program with the goal of becoming ABD (All But Dissertation); those are definitely not the initials you had in mind when you started this noble quest. A strong motivator for many doctoral students is money. By conservative estimates, you've probably invested at least $25,000 in your doctoral education. You would never dream of wasting that kind of money if you had it in your hand, so why would you throw it away by being ABD?

The dissertation is not easy, but it is certainly an opportunity for you to make all your hard work, time, and energy pay off. And while we're at it, let's focus on your investment of time. You have made an important investment in terms of the time you have put into earning your degree. You have voluntarily sacrificed time away from your family, missed vacations, spent late nights typing papers, and dedicated all those hours concentrating on your readings. In fact, if your time were converted to dollars, then your doctoral investment would equate to a much greater investment than the actual money you have spent.

Here is the good news—this is one investment where you don't have to worry about the stock market. You are in the driver's seat for making this investment pay off. You can do it, with a continued focus of time and effort. The return on this particular investment is all but guaranteed if you commit to finishing the dissertation. Your time, your money, your effort—they will all be worth it when you cross the stage at graduation.

One recommendation I have as you work on the dissertation is to find a partner or buddy who will commit to working with you in this endeavor. If your doctoral program uses a cohort model, you may already have someone from your group with whom you are close and who is in the same stage of candidacy. If so, choose a cohort member who is both committed to completing the dissertation and who will take this part of the process seriously. If you are not part of a cohort group, find someone from one of your doctoral classes or ask your dissertation chair for a recommendation if you don't know someone who would be a good fit.

Finding a "dissertation partner" makes it much easier to stay committed to the dissertation because you have someone else to whom you are accountable. Actually, you and your partner don't have to have similar topics, share similar methodologies, or even have the same chair. What's important is that you and your partner share a strong level of commitment and can set aside time each week to focus on dissertation work.

What if your dissertation "world" is not perfect and no support partner is available? I would recommend developing your own personal accountability system for completing the dissertation. Commit to working on the dissertation a certain amount of time each week, keep track of the time you spend, and evaluate whether or not you are living up to your own personal expectations.

Up to this point, you've established a great track record of achievement—you've successfully completed all your courses, and you've passed your comprehensive exams. Those are big accomplishments, big hurdles you have cleared. Now it's time to stretch and jump the final hurdle! Set monthly goals and establish a reward system for yourself for meeting your goals. Whether you choose a pedicure or dinner and a movie with friends, make your reward worthwhile. Be realistic when establishing your goals by bearing in mind that completing the dissertation is not a quick process and that sometimes "real life" can put speed bumps in your way.

Another way to avoid being ABD is to establish regular meeting times with your dissertation chair. Your chair is your friend in this process, your advocate, someone who is truly vested in your success. With that said, make sure that your chair knows how hard you are working. Speaking from my own experience as chair, I have multiple doctoral students working on their dissertations at the same time, so the person who keeps connected and works hard gets my attention.

It's in your best interest to stay closely connected with your chair and be responsive to any feedback. In fact, make a point of touching base with your chair at least every couple of weeks. Consistent feedback from your chair allows you to make revisions and corrections as you go along and will prevent you from feeling overwhelmed with a huge number of edits occurring at once. Furthermore, your chair can help you understand how the dissertation process works, as well as assist you in setting reasonable parameters and goals for completing the various stages of the project.

Unlike you, your chair actually has been through the dissertation process before, which makes him or her an invaluable resource for you in this unfamiliar territory. Without a doubt, your chair wants to see you finish the dissertation and be successful, so take advantage of your chair's expertise and willingness to help by staying in regular contact and incorporating all the feedback you are given. It will definitely have a big pay off for you in the long run.

One final word of advice about the dissertation: when those occasions surface where you simply think you'll never finish, remind yourself of why you started the doctoral program. I'm sure you had definite goals for undertaking the program and specific reasons why you pursued a terminal degree.

Periodically revisit these goals and reasons for taking on doctoral work. A regular dose of reflection never hurt anyone! In addition to personal growth and new learning, consider how the doctorate will afford you opportunities for advancement in your current career or offer other important professional options. For example, the options of teaching college classes, pursuing a career in academia, or expanding your resume with educational consulting are all opportunities that come from completing the dissertation and not being ABD.

I encourage you to prepare yourself for how the unknown might have an influence on your ability to complete your doctoral work. Whether you're working on your dissertation or not, there are times when real life happens. Unforeseen circumstances, usually beyond your control, can abruptly change your perspective. Serious personal incidents, family illnesses, divorces, or major changes at work are all examples of things that can prompt monumental shifts in momentum. If life happens, give yourself a break. Your dissertation should be a top priority, but there are times when it is reasonable to step back and refocus. If you are faced with a major life-changing event, you need to reassess the situation and determine what it will take to be successful. It may be that you need a few months away from the dissertation, and this is not necessarily a bad thing. Give yourself a specific timeline to cope, heal, and move forward, and then acknowledge that once that timeline has passed you will refocus on completing the dissertation.

Completing a dissertation is a tough, tedious, and time intensive experience. It is something you have never done before, something for which you have no real frame of reference. If it were easy to accomplish, many would have a doctoral degree. Indeed, that's not the case, and that's why finishing your dissertation will set you apart.

Completing the dissertation is a phenomenal learning experience, and perhaps most importantly, it's what separates those who have a doctoral degree from those who don't. It really is what makes you special. It's not easy, but I know you can do it. Work with your chair, hold yourself accountable, and set aside time each week (with or without a partner) to work on the dissertation just as you would for regular course assignments. Use these tools to complete the dissertation and reap the rewards of your investment. You have the ability, you have the tools, and you can make it happen. Most importantly, you deserve it.

11

When Motivation Hits Bottom

Dr. Connie L. Fulmer
University of Colorado–Denver

It happens when you least expected it—and you don't know why. The energy you once had to complete your dissertation has mysteriously vanished. You think you might walk away from it all—abandon your work and forgo data analysis. The motivation that you once had to complete this work has hit rock bottom.

There could be several reasons for low levels of motivation at this point in your journey. I will share some of them with you and you can decide which, among them, are contributing to your lack of forward progress. Understanding how motivation works will help you change your mindset, neutralize these negative perspectives, and put you back on a positive track. Do you know much about Vroom's (1964) Expectancy or VIE Theory, which maps performance to individual factors such as personality, skills, knowledge, experience, and abilities? These factors (valence, instrumentality, and expectancy) impact your level of motivation to achieve end goals—in this case, finishing that dissertation.

VALENCE

The first factor in VIE Theory is valence, or the strength of your preference to achieve a goal or objective among other competing goals. For the valence factor to be positive, you must prefer reaching the goal at a stronger level than not preferring to reach the goal. For instance, if you prefer to have something sweet at the end of a meal but the only choice is chocolate cake—and chocolate makes you sick—your motivation for something sweet is substantially reduced. If instead one of the choices is a banana split—and bananas are your favorite—your motivation for the sweet banana split may be stronger. Your desire for the banana split is so strong that you push to the front of the dessert line.

Like the dessert scenario, there may be several issues competing simultaneously for your attention during the dissertation process. The new baby, for example, or that part-time job you picked up to help pay the bills. Moreover, personal comments from a significant other or family members about "being tired of your seemingly perpetual-student status" are potent distractions. These competing distractions or stressors can easily reduce your preference or intention to complete your work. Think about which of these stressors, or perhaps others not mentioned, that are weakening your motivation to complete your dissertation.

INSTRUMENTALITY

The second factor in VIE Theory is instrumentality, or how achieving the first level outcome—completing the dissertation—will lead to other related secondary goals. In this case, completing the dissertation is instrumental in landing that faculty position in a prestigious university or a higher salary that comes with a new career. Sometimes you have to look beyond that first-level goal to secondary goals that are capable of leveraging more positive outcomes when completing the dissertation process. Perhaps you enjoy your graduate program to the extent that you don't want it to end. I remember feeling that way.

To increase your motivation for achieving the first level outcome, layer on extra secondary outcomes—construct six or seven of them! Begin to notice stressors that weaken your preference for achieving the first-level outcome. Then begin to think of additional secondary goals that you will accrue once you complete your work, adding to your motivation. These secondary goals will boost your motivation to complete your dissertation. Another strategy is to construct level-three goals once secondary goals are achieved.

These first two factors, valence and instrumentality, are important explanatory factors to help you discover why your motivation is either sky high or bottomed out. The good news is that you are in control of what you think. You choose either a positive or a negative path. Take a mental walk back through the past couple of weeks and see what might have happened emotionally to you regarding finishing your work. See if any of those incidents have impacted your enthusiasm for finishing your work or your desire for the other good things that will follow.

EXPECTANCY

The third factor in VIE Theory is expectancy, the belief that if you complete all the subtasks that lead to the eventual completion of your dissertation, you will reach the level-one goal. This means, for example, that you believe that if you begin the dissertation with a strong chapter that lays out the context of your work within the literature of the field and provides a rationale for how the work will make a contribution to your field, you will have completed one of the subtasks required for successfully completing your dissertation.

Similarly, you believe that if you review enough literature, you will find the right pieces to construct a literature review that is substantive and substantial—another requirement for a completed dissertation. You believe that if you write the methodology section with direction, clarity, and appropriate data collection procedures, you will have data to answer the research questions. If you analyze your data according to plans in the methodology chapter, you will convince your committee you are capable of conducting research worthy of the degree you are seeking.

And finally, you believe that if you are able to articulate all that you have learned through this dissertation process, the concluding chapter of your dissertation will provide evidence of your worthiness as a scholar. In sum, expectancy is the belief that if you are capable of completing all those individual subtasks, you will achieve that final goal—successfully defending your dissertation.

Sometimes students have little confidence that all these subtasks, when performed, will come together into the completed dissertation. Or, they don't have confidence that they can complete these subtasks because new stressors come to light. Have you lost confidence in the directions given by the chair of your committee? Are members of your committee playing out some battle that has little to do with you or your dissertation?

All of these stressors play havoc with the expectancy factor that supports the achievement of your level-one goal. This third factor is focused on your efficacy or confidence level in your skills, persistence, and capacity to work hard enough to complete these tasks.

FOCUSING ON THE POSITIVE

I know that your motivation to complete this work has bottomed out, but I also know that the answer to why this has happened is somewhere inside of you. You know that many believe in your capability to complete this work, but you are questioning whether or not you want to move forward. Expectancy Theory and the three factors of valence, instrumentality, and expectancy are powerful concepts to help you unpack reasons why your motivation is at rock-bottom levels.

It is my hope that the information presented in this chapter will help you to focus more positively on your capacity to complete this work. Asking and answering questions related to valence might help you refocus and move out of this malaise. What was your motivation to start this journey? What did you want to learn? How has the process enriched your life so far? Similarly, asking questions related to the concept of instrumentality may help bolster your resolve to complete your work. How many secondary goals will accrue to you once you complete this dissertation? How many level-three goals will follow those level-one and -two goals? And finally, ask yourself what part of the expectancy puzzle might be bothering you. Are any of these subtasks out of reach? Are you lacking skills in any of these areas? Is something not clear to you?

I believe that when you address these or other appropriate questions you will be able to refocus on all the positive benefits of completing your dissertation, not only for you but for future students whom you will support during their journeys at the academia. I expect that when you sort through these questions, high levels of motivation will return, and as a result, you will successfully defend your dissertation.

REFERENCES

Vroom, V. H. (1964). *Work and motivation.* New York: Wiley.

12

Passion: Don't Embark Without It

Dr. Megan Tschannen-Moran
The College of William & Mary

Writing a dissertation is a long, arduous journey that will require you to demonstrate a complex set of skills. To embark on such a journey without passion for your topic is like setting off to trek the Appalachia Trail wearing tennis shoes and carrying a day pack. You will be ill-equipped for the rigors of the task ahead, and it is unlikely that you will persevere to the end.

Completing a dissertation requires fortitude. There will almost certainly be bumps in the road, discouraging turns, and moments of feeling overwhelmed and just plain exhausted. If you get down this path with a topic that doesn't really interest you, that you don't care deeply about, it is going to be difficult to find the motivation to persevere through those rough patches. Being able to refresh yourself at the well of passion will help sustain you through the long journey ahead.

CONTRIBUTION

Consider the contribution that you hope to make through your dissertation. You don't want to overestimate the contribution your study will make, but you don't want to underestimate it either. This is not your life's work or the primary professional contribution you will make in your career.

A dissertation is a "beginner study," or what I like to call a research study with training wheels. In it, you will conduct independent research under the supervision and guidance of your dissertation chair and of your committee. However, neither is it insignificant in its potential to make a real and substantive contribution to the field.

To conduct a study of sufficient quality to earn your degree will require you to invest a year or more of hard effort—far too much time and effort for the end result to be that your committee members are the only people to hear about or care about your results (although their opinion is obviously crucial). You won't want your study to languish on a library shelf if you have designed a study that makes a substantive contribution to what we know about the complex processes of learning, teaching, and leading schools.

QUESTIONS

At the heart of a dissertation study are the research questions. These guide every aspect of the process, from the statement of the problem to the methods, all the way to the conclusion. A quality dissertation study requires starting with great questions. To be great, questions must meet two criteria—they must be both interesting and important.

An interesting question is one that is contestable, that is, it is not a settled issue upon which everyone more or less agrees. Unless there is something to argue about, you will have a hard time constructing a cogent argument as the rationale for your study in Chapter 1 of your dissertation. An interesting question means that it is something that you personally are curious about and that you are able to articulate your curiosity in a way that sparks other people's curiosity as well.

The "importance" criterion has to do with what difference it is likely to make to the enterprise of schooling when you offer evidence in answer to the questions you have posed. Education is an applied field, which means that we do not invest our energy in esoteric pursuits. We do research that assists educational organizations to do a better job of fulfilling their mission. Again, in making the case for your study in your Chapter 1, you will have a difficult time persuading your reader that your question is an important one if you are not convinced of this yourself.

FINDING YOUR PASSION

Many doctoral students find themselves in the situation of an abundance of curiosity and a lack of focus on any one particular topic that stands out as more important or more interesting than the rest. How then do you find your passion? One way is to map your own curiosity.

Throughout your doctoral studies, collect questions that occur to you as you read assignments or come away from class discussions. What stimulates you? What puzzles you? What makes you angry? What captures your imagination? As you review the questions you have collected, examine them with a researcher's eye. Where do you see themes and patterns of issues that you return to again and again?

Examine your history as an educator. Where have you invested your efforts and what endeavors have you found most rewarding? Examine your own heart. Notice instances of elevated energy and engagement, as these are symptoms of passion.

Elevated energy is not enough, though, if the issue that has your heart pumping is only of interest to you or to a small group of people. Do not select a topic to settle a personal score, to expose the misbehavior or misadventure of a single individual, or to process your emotions around an instance of betrayal. The length of time it takes to write a dissertation is a long time to steep you in the energy of revenge. You may well be over it long before the dissertation is complete, and you will be stuck rehashing that territory beyond what is helpful to you or to others. That story, although it may be filled with intense emotion for those most closely involved, is unlikely to be of value to the field as a whole. Even if it is an interesting story, with unexpected plot twist, intrigue, and treachery, it nonetheless does not likely meet the criteria of "important" in the sense that knowing the answers to the questions posed will assist schools to do a better job of fulfilling their mission to students.

To find a set of questions that matter to place at the heart of your study, imagine yourself on the other side of the dissertation. Imagine that you have the answers to the questions you have posed. Who would you tell? Who would be interested? Imagine yourself presenting your results at a conference. When you get up to say, "Hey World, look what I've found!" what are the kinds of findings you would hope to report? Imagine yourself publishing your results in a regional, state, national, or international publication. What are the practical and research implications from your study that you would be pleased to write about?

Writing a dissertation requires an enormous investment of effort and time. It is not only an investment in your learning as you hone the complex array of skills required to conduct educational research, it is an opportunity to make a contribution to the knowledge base of academia. Don't squander that opportunity by aiming too low, by playing it too safe, or imagining too small a contribution. Within the bounds of what is feasible, aim to make a substantive contribution. Strap on your boots, shoulder up your pack, and embark on an adventure to explore uncharted territory in the realm of interesting and important questions.

13

Brains, Heart, Courage, and Home: When Doctoral Students Have Significant Personal Issues Confounding the Completion of the Dissertation

Dr. Patrick D. Pauken
Bowling Green State University

For several years, I have had the privilege of chairing a multidisciplinary program in leadership studies at Bowling Green State University. The program attracts full-time and part-time students from a wide variety of professional fields: principalship, superintendency, curriculum and instruction, special education, counseling, school psychology, higher education, business, organizational development, health care, social work, government, law, and nonprofit organizational leadership. From a list of professions this varied, it is not a surprise that we meet and work with some amazingly diverse people from the region, the state, the nation, and around the world.

Each of these students shares common academic dreams: The recognition that leadership is universal, the advancement of knowledge in leadership studies, the contribution to theory and practice, and the ultimate completion of a doctoral degree. Their accomplishments and work ethic are humbling and inspiring. And their ability to realize these dreams is even more incredible in light of their "day jobs"—full-time professional positions in organizational leadership, obligations to family and community, and life in general.

Our program has graduated nearly 100 students in the past 10 years. Each of these fine people has a wonderful content and research methodology to contribute to academic and professional life. No doubt, the doctoral experience is filled with issues of coursework, exams, research proposals, logistics with registration and other student-based paperwork, dissertation committee chemistry, classmate chemistry, and the ultimate job hunt. Most often those issues are resolved in due course and with great success.

The doctoral experience is filled with significant stories and experiences that each student shares from his or her personal life. A short, representative list will offer a sampling of what we've witnessed in our program alone, although I suspect rosters of doctoral students from other programs would reveal the following as well: financial struggles, professional relocations, new jobs, lost jobs, children with special needs at home, deaths in the family, divorces, new babies, significant health issues, and a great opportunity to travel overseas with the Peace Corps. I recently said the following to one of our students, who claims he's "behind his classmates." "Behind what? Remember, this isn't a competitive race; it's a journey. You have a lot of work to do. But you're on the path and proceeding well. Besides, take a look at your last year: houses, spouses, children, and jobs. So I'll repeat, 'behind what?'"

At our doctoral orientation each fall, I take the new cohort through the program of study, but I like to do so with some catchy theme. In the fall of 2009, one of our recent graduates suggested *The Wizard of Oz* as the theme. Why not? It's a well-known book and movie. It sings. It dances. It moves from black and white to color. It's a journey with friends, both new and old. It confronts demons, both natural (tornadoes) and man-made (wicked witches). And it challenges aspects of our character that we only thought we didn't have with us the whole time.

So, you and Toto may not be in Kansas anymore. But, rest assured, you are not alone. You have brains, heart, courage, and the power to realize dreams and travel home.

BRAINS: POLICY, PRACTICE, AND PRODUCT

Doctoral students going through tough times, including experiences away from campus, have many options available for help and resolution. The "to-do" list of the doctoral student writing a dissertation may no longer include coursework and exams on set schedules. But the list is, nonetheless, long and complicated. For the "brains" of overcoming these tough times, I'll offer two pieces of advice.

First, consult the policies and practices for graduate education at your university. As unique as your issues may be, your graduate college or graduate school will likely be able to help. To start, universities will likely have a maximum number of years allowed to graduate. Most often your programs will be slated to take far fewer years. In other words, there is likely some built-in wiggle room. Check your graduate catalog and program handbook.

My guess is you have time to deal with personal crises and the doctoral degree, even if one set of issues has to take precedence for a while. On top of a published number of years to finish the degree, your university may offer an opportunity to petition for an extension, particularly in light of significant personal issues (e.g., prolonged illness). In fact, you may wish to check for the possibility of a leave of absence that would stop the clock for a certain period of time.

I have never met a doctoral student without an overflowing plate of things to do, particularly those who are working full time or raising families. Often, among the items on the to-do list, it's the dissertation that is the most flexible. There may be some dissertation-related items that can't be moved easily without a significant delay (e.g., data collection that must occur in a short window that is open only once each year). You may have to keep this item on the front burner.

Although I never wish to encourage slow-downs when a student is on a roll, it is all right for the dissertation to take a break from its author for a necessary time. And there may be some silver linings to such a decision, especially when life takes over. Please be good to yourself and attend to what's the most real and most important. Graduate colleges and academic programs have policies and practices that allow for such events. The dissertation will most likely be here when you get back. We promise.

Second, when it comes to dissertation and doctoral success, the brains of the operation belong primarily to one person: the student scholar. Never forget that. Even in the roughest of times—perhaps especially in the roughest of times—you should remember the knowledge base that got you this far. You would not be writing a dissertation if you weren't qualified to do so. You have worked hard to acquire the knowledge, language, and practice of your discipline. Have confidence in that. And use it well. Take comfort in your comfort zone. And remember to pick a manageable topic that you will still like at the end of the journey.

The yellow brick road to the Emerald City has its road blocks, detours, scary trees, and poppy fields. Lions, tigers, and bears, if you will. But good witches and munchkins have shown you the way with policy, practice, care, and shared knowledge. And you've picked up some knowledge of your own along the way. You'll make it.

HEART: IT'S ALL ABOUT RELATIONSHIPS

Perhaps the greatest thing about the doctoral experience is the source of its biggest trouble—independence. We work hard for years and obtain multiple degrees to earn the opportunity to explore a topic to its greatest depth and to have the open schedule to do so. Researchers on a quest for answers to society's great and necessary questions need the independence to travel where the questions and the data take them. This is, indeed, a great thing. But do not mistake your earned independence for a state of loneliness. Thankfully, independence and loneliness are not synonyms. Remember, you are not alone. In other words, please pay some attention to the people behind the curtains.

There are many people in your life waiting with open arms and receiving hearts: your friends and family, your dissertation committee, other program faculty and staff, your classmates, graduate student clubs and organizations, and, if needed, the university's counseling services. If significant personal issues burden you during your doctoral experience, reach out. We may not be experts in the particulars of the issues you are facing. But we have ears, eyes, shoulders, and open arms.

One of my favorite readings in ethical leadership is Lynn Beck's 1994 book, *Reclaiming Educational Administration as a Caring Profession*. In the first chapter, she presents three activities of caring: receiving, responding, and remaining.

Receiving is the caregiver's openness and willingness to accept another's reality uncritically. "To care for someone, I must know many things. I must know, for example, who the other is, what his powers and limitations are, what his needs are, and what is conducive to his growth" (Mayeroff, 1995, p. 340).

In responding, caring must go beyond knowing and into action. According to Beck, by equating care with an active concern for the life and growth of those we love, caring actions move in the direction of the growth and development of another.

Remaining calls for commitment, loyalty, responsibility, and sacrifice. I believe the best advisors, mentors, and friends accept and perform these three activities rather naturally. I speak with my own doctoral advisor at least once a week to this day. My law school advisor shared the greatest professional lesson I've learned. During my first year of law school, in my initial meeting with my advisor, he told me the following: "Remember, we're students and teachers for only a few years. We're friends and peers for life."

The success that comes from a doctoral experience is not found merely in the common experiences of coursework and examinations. Success is found in the lifelong relationships built among classmates. Even after coursework and exams, when cohort-mates move on to their dissertations, and where the questions and answers are more unique and focused, the cohort is still there. Never shy away from calling on your classmates. Chances are they need you, too. If your core courses met at a regular day and time, keep that time available and continue to meet with your cohort when needed. It may be more often than you think.

Even in the greatest depths of theory and research—in the stacks of the biggest library or on the umpteenth click of an Internet highway navigation—the story and the journey will always come back to the people in your life. It is all about relationships. Remember, there will always be someone nearby—with replacements for lost stuffing, an otherwise unreachable oil can, a well-timed ego boost, or a handshake and a hug.

COURAGE: NEVER FORGET WHAT (AND WHO) GOT YOU HERE—IT WILL GET YOU HOME

In a short passage in *Leading With Soul*, Bolman and Deal (1995) tell a sweet little story about leaning into one's fear. Two unnamed characters are having a conversation, one afraid of uncertainty ahead and the other celebrating it. The first character starts: "I want you to be my wizard. Give me the answers. You keep telling me to look inside. When I do, I hear the same voices. Be rational. Be in control. Be careful." The second character replies: "Those are messages from your head, not from your heart. It's hard to let go of old rules. It takes courage and faith. . . . Those woods go on for miles. Take a walk." (Bolman & Deal, 1995, pp. 47–48).

As much as your doctoral study is filled with a quest for knowledge and truth, it is also filled with uncertainty, including the uncertainty that comes from personal life. Know this going in. Be true to yourself—even in the face of new experience. Courage is the control of fear. In the end, it's more exciting than scary.

Do not forget what (and who) got you here in the first place. Just as it was with brains and heart, your courage brings you to the home stretch of dissertation writing. Robert Coles (2000), in *Lives of Moral Leadership*, tells the story of Al Jones, an African American parent in Boston in late 1960s, who stepped forward to drive a school bus into a newly desegregated city. Coles writes that a critical situation "can turn a seemingly ordinary person into someone bigger than he was, a leader, a moral leader" (p. 214). The best of our academic and professional leaders will maintain humility, but at the same time recognize and call on their strengths when needed most. De Marco (1996) speaks grandly of courage, but at the same time, reminds us that courage is already a part of each of us:

> [Courage is] the virtue that enables us to face firmly and undismayed the difficulties and dangers that stand in the way of duty and goodness. . . . Courage allows us to maintain our personal authenticity at times when surrendering to the familiar and secure is most inviting. (p. 47)

Spoken another way, despite the writing in the sky, Dorothy did not surrender. Brains, heart, courage, and home—she had them with her the whole time.

THERE'S NO PLACE LIKE HOME

> Why, anybody can have a brain. That's a mediocre commodity. Every pusillanimous creature that crawls on the Earth or slinks through slimy seas has a brain. Back where I come from, we have universities—seats of great learning, where men go to become great thinkers. And when they come out, they think deep thoughts and with no more brains than you have. But they have one thing you haven't got: A diploma. (The Wizard to the Scarecrow, *The Wizard of Oz*, 1939)

Doctoral students at the dissertation stage are, simply, too close to turn back. Remember the courage you had to apply to the program in the first place? Don't lose it now, especially when faced with significant challenges. You've made it through coursework and candidacy exams. You've mastered the content and the research methodology. If a significant personal matter takes you away from doctoral study for a time, please remember the strength of content and character that carried you this far. It will bring you back.

In the witch's castle, with the hourglass running low, Dorothy turns to the crystal ball, sees her Auntie Em, and the familiar musical theme returns. To all those who overcome unforeseen storms and find their way home, the dreams that you dare to dream really do come true.

REFERENCES

Beck, L. G. (1994). *Reclaiming educational administration as a caring profession*. New York: Teachers College Press.

Bolman, L. G., & Deal, T. E. (1995). *Leading with soul: An uncommon journey of spirit*. San Francisco: Jossey-Bass.

Coles, R. (2000). The bond between leaders and followers: Erik Erikson, Gandhi, and Albert Jones, a Boston bus driver. In *Lives of Moral Leadership* (pp. 204–226). New York: Random House.

De Marco, D. (1996). *The heart of virtue: Lessons from life and literature illustrating the beauty and value of moral character*. San Francisco: Ignatius Press.

The Internet Movie Database (n.d.). Memorable quotes for "The Wizard of Oz" (1939). Retrieved March 15, 2010, from http://www.imdb.com/title/tt0032138/quotes

LeRoy, M., & Freed, A. (Producers), & Fleming, V. (Director). (1939). *The wizard of oz* [Motion picture]. M-G-M.

Mayeroff, M. (1995). On caring. In C. Williams (Ed.), *On love and friendship: Philosophical readings* (pp. 170–205). Boston: Jones and Bartlett.

Schatán, M. (n.d.). Over the rainbow. Retrieved September 27, 2009, from http://www.papillonsartpalace.com/overtherainbow.htm

REDUCING, COPING, AND PREVENTING STRESS

This section of *The Doctoral Student's Advisor and Mentor* is dedicated to identifying stressors associated with a doctoral program. The contributors provide mentoring advice that speaks specifically to stress related to (a) doctoral studies, (b) tensions within professional relationships, and (c) programs examinations.

- Dr. Betty Merchant: Managing Your Stress
- Dr. Mary Frances Agnello: Eliminate Political Tensions With Your Dissertation Committee and Major Professor
- Dr. Rosemary S. Caffarella: Life Happens: So What Do I Do Now?
- Dr. Mark A. Gooden: Helping a Graduate Student Develop Self-Directedness in Stressful Times: A Brief Conversation
- Dr. A. William Place: Preparing for Qualifying Examinations

14

Managing Your Stress

Dr. Betty Merchant
University of Texas–San Antonio

In discussing stress, it's important to acknowledge that there is great variation in the way in which individuals experience and react to the events and circumstances around them. That is to say, what stresses you may not be perceived as stress by someone else. The experience of stress is deeply personal and intricately linked to your past experiences, beliefs, and dispositions. Having acknowledged this, my experience as well as that of the doctoral students with whom I have worked over the past 20 years, certainly indicate that the dissertation process is stressful for most individuals. The first part of this chapter suggests ways to minimize the self-induced stresses associated with writing the dissertation, and the second part provides suggestions about how to address the stress that remains.

A dissertation is often the first substantial research project that an individual undertakes and, as such, it is not reasonable to expect it to be comparable with the work of those who have been conducting research for years, as have the members of your committee. Consequently, the dissertation process is an apprenticeship of sorts, and you should be prepared to accept reasonable criticism of your work and to make the changes requested by the members of your committee. An exception to this would be a situation in which the changes requested actually result in seriously compromising the heart of your work, and in that case, I feel it's worth advocating for your position in a professional manner.

If you are unsuccessful in your attempt, it is generally a mistake and a serious loss of time to resist the advice of your committee members. Sometimes, however, there is one dissenting voice on a committee that is radically different from the others, and in this case, it may be best to replace the committee member with someone else. While this may feel uncomfortable at first, it will save a considerable amount of stress in the long run.

Another helpful way of minimizing self-induced stress is to approach the dissertation by writing in short segments (e.g., a three-page overview) and submitting it to your committee chair for review before investing any additional time in writing. Often, doctoral students attempt to undertake an unrealistic research task and resist attempts by their committee members to narrow the focus of their study.

One of the greatest stress producers is a situation in which a student, working in isolation, presents a 30- or 40-page document to the dissertation chair for a first-time viewing. Unpacking such a quantity of writing is almost always a miserable and painful process for both student and professor. It takes far longer to dissect something like this than it does to gradually build from a two- or three-page draft to a final product. Never attempt a significant amount of writing in the absence of feedback from your dissertation chair at each stage, and start off gradually with frequent reviews. This "slow but sure" method will definitely reduce stress and speed the time to completion.

The style of writing required of a dissertation is a specific academic style that is often difficult for people to master. Students who enjoy creative writing, for example, frequently complain about the restrictive nature of academic writing, and they experience a great deal of stress "bending" their writing styles to accommodate the preferences of their committee and the conventions of such academic style manuals.

Here I would like to change the focus from minimizing self-induced stress to suggestions for managing the stress that remains. One of the most common things students tell themselves during the dissertation writing process is that "When I'm finished with the dissertation, then I'll have the time to relax, the time to get back to the things and the people I've neglected during my doctoral studies." In fact, once you've successfully completed the dissertation, the kinds of new career opportunities that become available to you are usually highly demanding and associated with new kinds of stressors. The message is clear: Learn to manage stress as a doctoral student, because the career paths you are likely to choose after completing the dissertation will simply continue to challenge you and introduce you to new stressors.

At the risk of sounding overly simplistic, effectively managing stress requires a healthy and balanced approach to daily living. The dissertation process focuses on mental activity, and as such, is a boundless task. At some point, most dissertation students come to the difficult realization that there is no real limit to the time they could spend on it—that they could go on forever, searching the literature, gathering more data, doing more analyses, and so on. It's important to realize that there is no "off switch" in the dissertation process (other than your advisor, who is hopefully providing constructive limits to your activities in this regard).

This realization should be sufficient motivation for you to strike a balance between your dissertation-related activities and those that are essential to maintaining the other critical aspects of your life, including wellness and relationships. Neglecting any of these will most certainly create additional stress in your life and compound the dissertation-related stress you already feel.

Diet and exercise are vulnerable to the time pressures associated with the dissertation. The tendency is to resort to poor eating habits—not taking the time to eat healthy meals or eating too much of the wrong foods at the wrong time of day or night. Sitting at the computer has its own costs and contributes to physical and mental fatigue and such ailments as headaches, stiff necks, and shoulders. The lack of physical activity and the additive effects of muscle tension can be a devastating combination, one that becomes increasingly difficult to rectify.

I know of too many cases in which people rationalized their weight gain and physical inactivity by saying, "I got this way during the dissertation—when I'm done with this, I'll lose the weight I've gained" or "When this is over, I'll get back to healthy eating." It's amazing to watch how perfectly intelligent people can undermine their own health while creating an elaborate rational to justify their choices! Adopting a regular exercise routine is critical to stress reduction as well as to your overall health. In addition, mindfulness exercises (meditation or the like) can be an extremely powerful way of calming mind and body and increasing one's overall effectiveness.

Personal relationships can suffer during the dissertation writing process. A doctoral program often requires a large concentration of resources in the pursuit of a degree as well as a disproportionate burden on one's family and friends. Surrounded by fellow graduate students, it is easy to forget how isolating the experience can be for significant others in your life who are marginalized by the process. They often don't understand the specifics of the process, and, unlike your fellow doctoral students, are unable to understand the details of your experiences in the doctoral program or to serve as your professional confidants. One of the most poignant things I've heard from a doctoral student was: "I was in a real hurry to get this done, and I realized that I was neglecting my family in the process. I always told myself, that I'd get back to them when I was finished. Now I'm finished, and they're not there—my wife got tired of being overlooked and divorced me."

The bottom line: Organize your life during the dissertation as you expect to live it afterward, and in so doing, search for a balance in your life that optimizes your health, personal relationships, and professional development.

15

Eliminate Political Tensions With Your Dissertation Committee and Major Professor

Dr. Mary Frances Agnello
Texas Tech University

Marie, a doctoral student at the university, stopped by my office with a worried look on her face. She said that she was having trouble with her dissertation topic, and, more precisely, she was having difficulty in getting support from her chair for her desired topic. As it happens, my office is next door to her chair's office. So I invited Marie to come to my home on Sunday evening for a cookout. That way, we could have this discussion in an informal setting. The following is the dialogue that ensued in my backyard during a cookout one summer evening.

Dr. A: What can I serve you to drink, Marie? How are things going with your doctoral work?

Marie: I finished my coursework a year ago, and I cannot pin down my dissertation topic.

Dr. A: What would you like that topic to be?

Marie: I don't know exactly, but I would like to do some work around the concept of addressing diversity.

Dr. A: What is your area of expertise?

Marie: I am a science educator, but I have no desire whatsoever to do a dissertation around the topic of science education.

Dr. A: Why is that? It is such a hot topic.

Marie: I am sick of it. I have taught science for years. It is not the problem of teaching and learning science that I would like to explore, but rather something more fundamental.

(Walking over to the smoking pit—smelling good!)

Dr. A: Fundamental in what way?

Marie: I just see so many students, Hispanics in our part of the state in particular, who are just lost. They do not know how to make decisions about their learning. They do not have a sense of how to self-evaluate their needs and desires. They lack drive and interest in school in general, yet they want to succeed.

Dr. A: Why do you suppose that they do not know how to get their minds around academic work? And how might you address this topic in your dissertation?

Marie: I think it is fundamental failure on the part of the school to engage students in a feeling of being empowered about their learning and making decisions that will affect their lives. I have spoken to my chair about this issue and he says it is not a good idea to study diversity in a dissertation study.

Dr. A: What did he say?

Marie: He believes that it is too difficult to measure how the students have or have not been inspired over the years in the schools, and it is too difficult to do a quantitative measure of the foundational issues I am trying to study.

Dr. A: Well, how do you propose to study it? What have you read? What kind of study could you replicate?

Marie: I have read almost all of the big names in diversity—Gay, Ladson-Billings, Valenzuela, Nieto, Hernandez-Sheets, and more. I did not read about one specific study that I wish to replicate.

Dr. A: Well, how would you like to study what you are calling "foundational issues" in a way that would be first—doable, second—meaningful to you, and third—something that will make a contribution to the field and net you something from which you can publish an article or so?

Marie: I think I would like to do a qualitative study. But the kind of qualitative research that I would like to pursue does not seem to meet the approval of my chair.

Dr. A: What kind of qualitative study would that be?

Marie: A phenomenology . . . I don't know . . . something that would capture events, feelings, emotions, thoughts . . .

Dr. A: Have you told this to your chair?

Marie: Yes, I did. I was discouraged from doing anything other than a straight case study or a quantitative study.

Dr. A: Did you explore the possibilities of a quantitative study as your chair has described or prescribed?

Marie: Yes, I have. I just am not getting excited about anything that I read.

Dr. A: Have you read any dissertations on similar or related topics?

Marie: Yes, I found three in particular that seem to each have a component that might be appropriate for what I am trying to do.

Dr. A: Did you show the dissertations or components to your chair?

Marie: I did.

Dr. A: And . . .

Marie: I got the same response that I have just told you. He said, "You really need to do something that is a straight case study or a quantitative study."

Dr. A: And did you ask why?

Marie: I did.

(I am serving hamburgers and grilled veggies as we continue to talk.)

Dr. A: And what was the response?

Marie: The same thing I told you.

Dr. A: Have you spoken to other members of your committee?

Marie: Yes.

Dr. A: What did they say?

Marie: They advised me to do what my chair specifies, and they would support in any way that they could.

Dr. A: Is there any way that one of the other committee members could be your chair?

Marie: Not if I want my chair to stay on my committee.

Dr. A: Have you exhausted other possibilities of thinking about how you want to pursue this doctoral degree and more specifically the dissertation?

Marie: Yes, I have considered just re-forming my committee.

Dr. A: And do you wish to do that?

Marie: I don't know what to do at this point. I am just tired. I feel trapped. I cannot go forward; I cannot go backward. I am getting nowhere and I just need some help to figure out what I want to do.

Dr. A: I am sure that almost all doctoral students have felt the same emotions at one time or another during their programs. So, that is not unusual. What is problematic is that you cannot really make any progress until your chair is satisfied. This could mean that you may need to change chairs or do what your chair advises.

Marie: I do not feel right or good about either but I know that I am going to make a decision soon.

Dr. A: What have you considered as an alternative to the route you are currently on?

(Now, we are getting seconds. Food is a success!)

Marie: I have asked my chair if it would be too much a problem if I changed my committee and made someone else the chair.

Dr. A: And what was his response?

Marie: He turned really red and started shaking.

Dr. A: Oooooh, that's not good.

Marie: I know. I just hate stepping on people's toes and hurting feelings and being a problem to everyone.

Dr. A: Well, in case no one has reminded you lately, you are the client—the student. You are paying for this education and this degree. What you want is important. What you wish to do for your big study is something that will have enduring effects on you as a professional and as a human being. The dissertation often defines your professional trajectory for several years. It does not have to. But you have invested so much time in reviewing the literature and thinking about a topic that is meaningful to you, that it is difficult to do it again with the same intensity, and with the prospect of finishing in the next year and a half or so.

Marie: I know. And of course, money is an issue. And, now I am a single mother after having become a graduate student.

Dr. A: Yes, I know about those problems. You really need to finish; however, you need to produce a quality study and one that has meaning for you. I do remember the turmoil and conflict I endured during the time frame in which you find yourself. You have spent too much money and time to turn back now and you have a child to support whether you finish or not. If you finish, chances are you can provide more financial stability for her than if you leave ABD (All But Dissertation). ABD is not an option for you.

Marie: Yes, I feel so overwhelmed and up against a wall.

Dr. A: I would advise making a list—an outline if you will. Outline the project that you want to do and with whom it is doable. If your chair is not someone you can work with or anyone else on your committee, for that matter, you can make changes. It is not easy. It is not even necessarily advisable. (Reaching for a soft drink.) It is, however, of utmost importance that you figure out where you are going, what you need to do to get there, and how you plan to arrive at the desired destination.

Marie: I just hate to alienate people with whom I have worked.

Dr. A: I know. It is not a good situation . . . but neither is being ABD . . . nor being unable to support yourself and pay back your student loans.

Marie: So, if the committee ends up looking totally different and I can pursue my phenomenological study, it will be okay?

Dr. A: Well, you might lose a mentor and a friend. It might even come back to haunt you in your professional career. But I believe that it comes down to an ethical question. What do you need to do to finish your mission?

Marie: Will I be okay if I alienate people and then they work against me later in my career?

Dr. A: Will you be okay if you never finish? And have no career? And have no one to work with you in your future as an academic?

Marie: Well, I guess, since you put it that way, I really need to come up with a plan and then talk to all of my committee members and get my ducks in a row.

Dr. A: That is right. You need to have a plan and you need to proceed in a way that is meaningful to you and to your work.

Marie: Wow, I am really glad that I asked to discuss this with you. I feel better already, but I know I have a lot to do.

Dr. A: Yes, the best is yet to come! And it will!! (Lifting her diet soda to toast Marie.)

16

Life Happens: So What Do I Do Now?

Dr. Rosemary S. Caffarella
Cornell University

As we all know, life's interruptions such as birth, death, and illness are a part of the everyday lives of adults. Whether they are chosen or just happen, often at a crucial junction of a major task you have undertaken, such as a dissertation, times can get tough in so many ways—from emotional swings to physical pain. I remember well in my early 30s, a week before my own dissertation defense, I started to have major adnominal pains and found myself in the hospital 2 days later for major surgery. The doctor offered to write my advisor a note to excuse me from the defense, but I said I probably just needed to call, which I did.

My advisor, Professor Russell Kleis's response was that there would be no problem—we would just reschedule it. Of course then I had to tell him it would be at least 7 weeks before I could travel to Michigan from the East Coast. Russ's level of empathy, care, and support was so helpful because I was not only scared of this sudden medical procedure, but I was also disappointed that I could not defend my dissertation. I truly felt like I was ready (and just wanted to get it over).

Russ's response has stayed with me throughout my career as a professor and has served as a model for me in the way I react to students who find themselves in situations that they never imaged would happen anytime during their dissertation, which tends to be such an intense and often stressful time. It is a story that I have shared often and will continue to share with my graduate students.

I really do not want to reveal this observation upfront, but almost all of my doctoral advisees, and there have been many, have found themselves in crises during the process of writing their dissertations. These periods of change, whether turbulent or not, may bring students to a standstill in how they are able to react versus knowing what they should be doing—working on their dissertation. Some people are frozen in space and time, others move and make progress as a reaction to the crises, and still others are someplace in between.

Through the sharing of three stories, I provide examples of personal situations my students found themselves in during their dissertation processes. Each had different reactions, depending on who they are, the seriousness of the crisis, if the event came with some warning or none at all, and how they responded "when life happens."

I believe strongly that as an advisor my role is to listen, empathize, be willing to tell about my own experiences (if they relate), and most of all let them know that no matter what path they choose to take related to their work that it is okay. I can assist them with the decision-making process, but I can't make the decision for them. Oh, and yes, doctoral students do make it through crises and all.

The kinds of relationships that are needed to allow students space during the dissertation process to address their personal lives can be built even before students are formally admitted to a program. For example, before Steve was even admitted to our doctoral program he ran into a series of blocks. The university I worked at during this time required that students earn two semesters for residency requirements, which in essence means that the student has to be enrolled in full-time study.

Steve had started his work as a part-time student, taking one course a semester, and I acted as his "unofficial advisor." He was finally granted a year's leave of absence from his job, and then the spring before he was to enroll full time, his wife contracted a serious illness. There was no way Steve could leave his job at this time because he would lose his health benefits. The next year Steve was again granted another leave, but his work situation called for more responsibilities, and his organization put off his leave for another year.

Now Steve was more worried because he had to start full time the next academic year because if he did not, his earlier credits would not count toward the degree. I continued throughout that year, along with others in the department, to support him, including encouraging him to apply to other universities where he could complete his program part time or through alternative formats.

On his third try, Steve was finally granted his leave of absence, even though his supervisor did not want to let him go as he was too valuable to the organization. I then became his "official" advisor, for which both of us were delighted, and set the stage for a productive and collegial relationship as Steve moved quickly into his comprehensive examinations and dissertation phase.

Even though Steve encountered additional personal issues while working on his dissertation, the relationship we had built during the admissions phase, which was both collegial and valued by each of us, carried us through to graduation. We worked together well as mentor and mentee as well as colleagues and learned a great deal from each other, which is one of the joys of doctoral level advisement.

Heather's story relates directly to the dissertation phase of her program, but begins as soon as she was admitted. Although she was extremely bright and capable, she lacked the personal belief that she really belonged in a doctoral program. This feeling is not unusual, often referred to as "the imposter syndrome," that is students asking why they were admitted to a doctoral program (Brookfield, 1990).

For most students, these feelings go away as they experience success, but for Heather, she seemed to carry them with her no matter how well she did in her coursework or on her comprehensive exams. It seemed to be especially prevalent when Heather hit a rock wall in her personal life, which unfortunately she had more than her share of while working on her dissertation (Caffarella, 1993, 1996).

Changes in her life ranged from losing her dad, coping with a series of illnesses, and finding herself overcommitted by her inability to just say "no." Heather needed some personal space, especially when the losses hit, and a time for healing both physically and spiritually, as each of these issues took a lot out of her. I spent a lot of time just listening to her stories and helping her to feel that she was really not a failure because she perceived she was moving so slowly during her dissertation process.

Of course, there were rock walls with the dissertation process as well, as there usually is, in terms of executing the study, such as "Where and how do I get the right and enough subjects?" and "Am I on target with answering my research questions through the design I choose" (with assistance from her committee)? Heather felt pressured because she got married during this phase of the program and did not want to hold up her husband from his "dream job," which may have meant moving away as she was struggling to complete the process.

I give Heather a lot of credit for hanging in there, and I was glad that as her advisor I could support her in both her academic pursuits and her personal life, as it was extremely important for her to complete her doctorate. Although it took more time than she ever thought, the time was well spent. The contributions she made to our field of study have been exciting and appreciated by those who have been affected by her actions, and she has touched so many lives in such a positive way.

Jan found herself in a different sort of situation, one involving her demanding work life, coupled with an advisor, that is, me, who moved 2,000 miles to a new institution into a high pressure position while Jan was completing her dissertation. She, thank goodness, was highly committed to completing her doctoral degree for both personal satisfaction and job advancement or a move to a new kind of position still within the same field. Jan was self-directed in her learning—that is—she managed her time well and knew what she was doing, but still she had to continually juggle this conflict between her job commitments and the time it was taking to complete her study.

This time commitment was a mix—the research design Jan had chosen was difficult to execute, and gathering and analyzing her data were time-consuming endeavors. We met more often while I still lived in the area, either in the city where she lived and worked or at the university, which was an hour and a half drive away. She also had another conflict, which was personal in nature. The focus of her study was the workload of middle managers in hospital settings, and she was in the business of educating people who aspire to move into these positions.

Jan's assumption going into the study, through personal experience and her present position, was that the work pressures on this level of manager were unrealistic. Jan, therefore, felt an ethical dilemma in terms of knowing the field had a shortage of people needed for these positions, while at the same time, she was not only training but also encouraging her students to move into positions, even though she knew these jobs had a high potential for causing disruption in their personal lives.

Although Jan did not allow this personal dilemma to get in the way of her study, we often talked about it and how to incorporate these feelings and her observations into her study. This incorporation was important as she had chosen phenomenology as her study design. We worked out realistic time schedules, or ones we thought were realistic, and then reworked them more than once, so she could have a time frame in mind in terms of managing her own time. My moving across the country of course did not ease the situation, but it was helpful that I had experience working with students who either themselves had moved or because I had moved to another institution while advising them.

This knowledge was helpful to both of us, as working across long distances had worked well for me before. Using email, reviewing of drafts via computer, and telephone conferences proved productive. In addition, as my daughter and grandchildren lived in the area, when I was back to visit I made a point to meet with her and other advisees I had in the same situation. What was critical in making this situation work was that Jan was willing, able, and highly committed to complete her work, and I, in turn, was highly invested in her being able to complete an excellent study, which Jan did.

Where my stories lead to are four suggestions to ensure that in choosing a dissertation advisor you find a person you feel comfortable working with and who can provide solid academic advice, while at the time understands and works within the realities of our personal lives. Although for many students the dissertation advisor will probably not be selected until they are well into the program, you should look for these qualities in the faculty members when selecting a doctoral program:

- Choose an advisor who is competent in that she knows her subject well, accepts a variety of ways of looking at research problems and ways of studying them, and knows what it takes for novice researchers (Merriam, Caffarella, & Baumgartner, 2007), which most doctoral students are, to complete an excellent piece of research and address significant problems (Caffarella & Barnett, 2000).
- Ensure your advisor is a bright, caring, and ethical person, with a sense of humor who can laugh as well as carry on rigorous academic discussions about your work.
- If you determine you are not a match with your advisor (for example, in terms of your final focus area or methodology, unforeseen personality

clashes) is he or she willing and able to assist you in finding a better match for another advisor?
- Allow yourself to be a colleague of your advisor in a quest for knowledge that makes a meaningful contribution to your discipline or field of study.

You and your dissertation advisor probably will not become friends, although friendships do develop because of this experience and further professional involvement after graduation. The hope is that you will leave your experience of writing a dissertation feeling positive and good about what you were able to produce and having a mutual respect and caring relationship with your dissertation advisor. This relationship may mean exchanging holiday greetings or emails over time to sharing fond memories of a worthwhile experience that if you become a dissertation advisor you would want to carry over to students you mentor.

REFERENCES

Brookfield, S. D. (1990). *The skillful teacher.* San Francisco: Jossey-Bass.
Caffarella, R. S. (1993). The continuing journey of our professional lives. *Adult Learning, 4*(5), 27, 30.
Caffarella, R. S. (1996). Can I do it all? *Adult Learning, 8*(1), 8–9.
Caffarella, R. S., & Barnett, B. G. (2000). Teaching doctoral students to become scholarly writers: The importance of giving and receiving critiques. *Studies in Higher Education, 25*(1), 39–52.
Merriam, S. B., Caffarella, R. S., & Baumgartner, L. M. (2007). *Learning in adulthood. A comprehensive guide* (3rd ed.). San Francisco: Jossey-Bass.

17

Helping a Graduate Student Develop Self-Directedness in Stressful Times: A Brief Conversation

Dr. Mark A. Gooden
University of Texas–Austin

The following is a conversation between Starla Student, a doctoral candidate, and Dr. Stellar Mark, a professor in educational administration. While it is fictitious, it is based on an amalgamation of true events. It is only a snapshot of the many meetings I have had in the past, but it presents some of what I have learned over the years in dealing with doctoral students who are stressed because they take on too much.

I hope there is a lesson here for doctoral students and for professors. I hope it will present some ideas about how professors can approach their work in supporting students on the fertile plane of learning, which needs to prevail, but often competes with all the other stressors in a student's life.

Dr. Mark: How are you today?

Starla: I am really stressed.

Dr. Mark: What's going on?

Starla: Wow! Where do I start? Well, I have been struggling to adhere to my timeline but things keep happening in life that prevent me from doing that. I recently moved my aging mother in with me because she needed the additional support, financially, physically, emotionally, and otherwise. My mother is a pleasant person but she is losing her independence and that's been a challenge. Of course taking a leave from work last year left me with less money. Now, I have learned that I have to support her financially and I am feeling like I am in need of emotional support as I work to help her and complete my dissertation.

I am afraid my graduate assistant stipend will not get us through so I am going to be applying for some loans. That's been interesting dealing with financial aid. My son is having some issues at school. I have been out there several times and his teachers are just not supportive of him in my opinion. He's an active boy and needs to be engaged, but his teacher insists on thinking of him only as a "busy, though not rambunctious," African American kid who could probably benefit from some medication.

I suppose all doctoral students have challenges, but mine have left me drained emotionally, right when I need my energy the most. While I still want to get my degree, I am afraid that I am just not as focused as I was when I started 2 years ago. Much has changed since then, but I did not think I would be having this much trouble getting through. After all, I have been an award-winning teacher and an effective principal.

I started a tutoring program for the neighborhood kids around my church, and I have a strong commitment to continue that work as it helps so many of those students of color who are marginalized every day. That program is doing so well but the growth of it is demanding more of my time. I know I am not taking classes and you have said that I should be consistently working on my dissertation, perhaps a little each day, but I keep getting pulled away and the days are flying by. I am really feeling so stressed and overwhelmed that I believe a meltdown is imminent.

Dr. Mark: Take a deep breath. Now exhale. There's definitely a lot going on in your life right now. Wow! I got tired just listening to the list of many activities that you are engaged in and I think there are some things you did not mention. First, you should acknowledge that this is not an easy process and then think about what must change in your thinking and actions to balance all of the new changes in your life.

Naturally, that may require that you reconsider your timeline. It is likely going to take more time than you originally anticipated, and if it does, know that that's okay. However, be careful not to take on too many things, thereby making it impossible to finish in a reasonable time. That might be avoidance of the task at hand. Note that it is your timeline so you can change it, especially if it means keeping your sanity. How can I support you?

Starla: Do you have any suggestions?

Dr. Mark: Well, yes, I do. May I share them with you?

Starla: Sure.

Dr. Mark: Do you remember what you were thinking when you made the bold move to take time off to pursue your doctorate full time after 2 years of taking coursework? As I recall, you thought that it was going to be really tough, but you realized, in time, that it was the best move. What drove you to do that?

Starla: My commitment to do this work. My priority was to do it now and not put it off any longer.

Dr. Mark: Well it seems to me that you will have to prioritize even more now. You are going to have to decide what's important to you and then put your energy there. That means you will have to let some other things go for now, or perhaps forever. It may be helpful to write some of this down and see where you are spending your time. Do a sort of inventory and see what's getting most of your time and determine if it's really important to you.

I hope your studies will be a part of that list of top priorities when you finish this process. However, I doubt if you will be able to maintain the same pace and level of commitments and do everything well, or at all. Plus, you will be really, really stressed out and I know that's not how you do your best work. While I believe you are a good writer, I know you need a lot of time to do the work for your dissertation.

Again, that's a decision you have to make. I know you can complete your dissertation. I know you are involved in important roles with multiple organizations and that's important to you. Are those activities more important than completing your dissertation? Do you really need to do everything you are doing right now?

Starla: I think taking the inventory is a good idea. Thanks! However, I am not sure what I can drop right now. I suppose the inventory will help me answer that.

Dr. Mark: Do you think it's a good idea to try to keep everything?

Starla: No, but I have obligations to many people. Is this normal? Will my committee members think I am a slacker? I believe I am working hard to fulfill my role as an African American woman in the academy that is not always friendly to people of color. Whether it is real or perceived, I sometimes feel as if there were some who see me as inadequate. I realize that I should not be responding this way to what people think, but in the context of everything else, strangely, I find myself challenged a great deal by that kind of behavior. I want to do good work and I want to move ahead and get a job as soon as possible.

While I have thought seriously about the assistant professor position and I know that's what I really want to do, I am not sure that's going to be the route for me, especially when my former district is pulling on me to consider taking a job in the central office. The pay is much better too and my family could really use a financial boost now.

Dr. Mark: While all doctoral students have challenges, I would agree that there are unique challenges for African American doctoral students. Clearly, I owe a large part of my success as a professor in the academy to professors of color who were really willing to share their experiences in the academy, including triumphs and failures, and hard lessons learned along the way.

What I learned is that you have to build a support system and get at least one trusted mentor. While I can share some things, there are others who have different experiences that can inform your decisions. For instance, there are single mothers in the academy and they can offer advice that I simply cannot. You should ask them about their experiences and how they made it through.

It's tough comparing salaries of new assistant professors to those of experienced and even new prekindergarten to 12th-grade administrators. This decision is made even tougher for a doctoral student like you because you are the breadwinner in your household. However, you have to make the decision that's best for you and your family in the long run. That may require you postponing going into the professorate. I hope it does not, but that's not my decision to make. There are scholars who went back to the practitioner's world and then returned to academe later. While it might be harder to return later, it is not impossible.

Keep in mind that the professorate may not offer as much money initially but it can afford you a quality of life that gives you more control of your time. This may be helpful as you focus broadly on ways to support your family. Whatever route you take, you will need to do that soon because the preparation is different if you decide to go into the professorate. In fact, I believe, preparation for the assistant professor position starts much earlier in your doctoral program as it demands that you take on research projects and other activities that will lead to publications, the coin of the realm in academe.

Even though this is a hard and stressful choice to make and one that you have put off for a time, I encourage you to make it now. You must choose your path and travel it without trying to please everyone, including me. I am here to support you and will do that, regardless of the path you choose.

Dr. Mark: I have a question for you. Do you think things would be less stressful if *you* made that choice?

Starla: Perhaps.

Dr. Mark: Are there things we can do to make your life more manageable from our end?

Starla: I know you always say read through the graduate handbook and policies, and I do that. However, I think conversations with groups of professors about their experiences might be really helpful. Students could perhaps listen to professors share their experiences of going through their doctoral programs. I think this kind of advice would be really helpful. I would benefit in general but especially if professors of color could share, considering the small percentage of people of color in the academy.

It's weird but once you see how some people who look like you have overcome some of the same challenges, you don't feel as isolated. Moreover, I would want to know how they addressed some of the situations I am experiencing that are unique to young scholars of color.

Dr. Mark: I see. I actually received support from professors of color in the PROFS (Providing Research Opportunities for Future Scholars) program. Yes, that's an acronym! This was a wonderful program that really introduced us to what it meant to be a scholar of color. Listening to their stories helped us gain insight, so while the prospect of becoming a professor stressed us out in some ways, we knew exactly what we were getting into and felt supported in that decision. I will do some homework on that one and see what we can do. Don't be afraid to ask me about the progress in a few weeks.

Starla: Great! Listen, I have to go to pick up Jamel. This has been helpful. I feel more compelled to do what I have known for some time. I will appreciate your asking how things are going in the upcoming weeks. That will help me stay accountable.

Dr. Mark: I can do that. Listen, it was good seeing you. Please say hello to Jamel. Keep doing good work. You belong here and you are going to work this out.

18

Preparing for Qualifying Examinations

Dr. A. William Place
University of Dayton

The comprehensive examination is an important quality-control measure that most doctoral programs have in place for all students. Normally, it is not a review exercise in which the candidate reiterates information. They are not meant to be some kind of a group of final exams for your courses; rather, the examination is an attempt to assess the candidate's facility to:

- Demonstrate command of the literature in the area(s) tested,
- Demonstrate the ability to integrate the knowledge of a given area with that of another area(s),
- Demonstrate the ability to think critically (i.e., to interpret, apply, analyze, synthesize, or evaluate),
- Integrate disparate information,
- Respond creatively and critically to the issues raised,
- Conduct and analyze research, and
- Communicate these matters in a scholarly manner.

As with so much doctoral work, a great deal depends on the specifics of your institution. For example, the policy at this specific institution is that exams are given only twice a year, and that all students are given the same exams, which have been evaluated by three-member subcommittees in each of the three areas (there is an attempt to keep the evaluation blind in that students are given a number and the evaluators do not see the student name).

As is common at many institutions, students write for 4 hours a day for 3 days. For this institution, each day is designated for an academic area (i.e., the first day is research methods and design, the second is for core/foundations, which includes organizational theory and change as well as ethics, and the third day is the concentration, which for this institution is either higher education administration/leadership or PreK–12 administration/leadership). Other institutions give individually tailored exams to each candidate and do not attempt to make the evaluation blind.

It is important for candidates to know the policy of who will assess their answers and what options or results can be the consequence of that assessment. For example, the student's individual committee may assess the exam or there may be a committee of faculty used for all students. The options may vary, but common ones are to first determine if the student failed that area and if they would (a) need to rewrite, (b) write a scholarly paper, (c) have an oral exam, (d) retake one or more courses, or (e) a combination of these alternatives. It is common for universities to have severe consequences if the second attempt is deemed unsuccessful (i.e., students are removed from the program).

With such pressure, it is important to take the comprehensive exam process seriously. Start preparation early and, although individual classes are not just reexamined, know the major areas and those that relate to the classes you take. Keeping the texts and notes can be helpful as you prepare.

I recommend beginning at least 6 to 8 months prior to the test date with serious and consistent time blocks committed specifically to your preparation for the comprehensive exams. Some programs provide sample questions and some even allow students to see copies of some of the previous exam questions. If this is available, use these as you start to study.

You should find out about the actual administration conditions. In many universities you are expected to be able to answer questions without any resources, connection to the Internet, or written material. Know what is the role of the proctor—he or she may be able to provide technical support for you in relation to the computer, but not answer questions about content. Some institutions will allow you to correct spelling and grammar after the actual writing, provided you do not make any substantive changes or additions.

In my own preparation, I found that a student-organized study group was invaluable. This is the single most common strategy and is extremely helpful, but students must take personal responsibility for their own preparation. Individuals can compare notes and thoughts, but division of labor can be problematic (e.g., if you rely on another student's synopsis of organizational theory, you are likely to have a difficult time integrating the concepts sufficiently to demonstrate your mastery of the material).

These groups can be good if there is a real and honest critique of one another's work. Using sample questions (if they are available—if not the group should attempt to develop their own sample questions), you should develop what you believe to be good answers. Then ask others to critique your answers frankly. For the first few efforts, you may want to use all available resources until you get a good feel and become comfortable constructing scholarly answers, but you should quickly transition to simulate the actual exam situation.

As a way of demonstrating a command of the field and the literature, you should be able to cite the prominent authors on a topic and integrate their positions into your answers. However, you should do more than list authors and positions—you need to demonstrate you are ready to enter the dialogue of the community of scholars.

Personally, I was quite concerned about the physical task of getting my thoughts on paper during a 4-hour time period, and the first couple of practice times the muscles in my hands actually felt cramped by the end of the 4-hour period. It was important to find that out and then to work each week for several months so that I got to the point where that physical limitation was no longer a concern. It may well have been more of a mental limitation because of the need to think as you write (or type), but it felt real to me and the practice made me feel comfortable with the task by the time I took the exam.

Each person needs to be aware of his or her own test approach, and just as PreK–12 practitioners have become aware of how to lower the students' anxiety in relation to the high-stakes test those students take, you need to be relaxed enough to perform at your highest level for your high-stakes comprehensive exam.

The advice to sleep well, eat well, and use stress-relief mechanisms applies. Sleep is difficult for many and each person is different, but you should try to develop a pattern of getting to sleep at a consistent time and then waking up at a consistent time. This can take months to get your body adjusted to, so again do not wait until 2 or 3 weeks before the date to start adjusting your sleep patterns. I have a habit of using short "power" naps to help me be productive in the afternoon and evening, but if the exam is administered in the morning, you may wish to avoid these naps for a number of months prior to the date of your comprehensive exam.

Doctoral programs can be a bit of an emotional roller coaster. A positive attitude is sometimes difficult to keep, but it is perhaps the most important aspect of your preparation to maintain. The preparation for this experience is part of what will make you a stronger professional.

Most students have become good at repeating what a particular faculty member expects on a final or in a term paper, but this exercise is quite different and although not necessarily a fun activity while you are doing it, the breadth and depth of what is expected can be truly transformative. When you were admitted into the program, you agreed to meet the challenge of academia; and faculty really do hope to see students succeed and achieve great things. Therefore, relax and show the scholarly potential your mentors hope to see in you.

IV

LIFE AFTER THE DOCTORATE: OPPORTUNITIES FOR ADVANCING YOUR CAREER

This section of *The Doctoral Student's Advisor and Mentor* is dedicated to career advancement for the doctoral student. The contributors' mentoring advice provides the doctoral student with strategies to advance their career.

- Dr. Michelle D. Young: Using Your Dissertation as a Steppingstone to a University Faculty Position
- Dr. Charles L. Slater and Mtra. Gema López Gorosave: Using the Dissertation as a Vehicle for Publishing: A Conversation Between Professor and Doctoral Student
- Dr. George Theoharis: Maximizing Your Dissertation to Propel Your Career
- Dr. Catherine Lugg: What Do You Want to Do With This? Means-Driven Dissertation Writing

19

Using Your Dissertation as a Steppingstone to a University Faculty Position

Dr. Michelle D. Young
The University of Texas–Austin

If you are thinking seriously about a career as a professor, you are in for a stimulating and satisfying experience. To begin your career in the strongest position possible, it is important that you understand what experiences you should have as a graduate student in addition to your course and dissertation work. Although it is always important to be flexible and open to emerging opportunities, it is also important to plan your path from graduate school to the professoriate.

If you have just started your doctoral program, you are likely to have a lot on your mind, including what you plan to do as a result of earning your doctorate. Obviously, there are many choices. You could continue doing what you were doing prior to entering a doctoral program or you could use the doctorate to move to a new and hopefully more prestigious position. For some, like me, the choice to earn a doctorate is a choice to enter academe.

I will never forget my days as a doctoral student at the University of Texas–Austin. I had entered a brand new program in educational policy with a small, close-knit group of students, all of whom were planning to enter academe as faculty members. We did not have this book as a resource, but we did have excellent mentors who helped us navigate the field and enter the professoriate with useful experiences and a competitive record.

Based on my experience working in and with faculty in primarily research-extensive universities in the United States, mentoring graduate students, serving as references for job candidates, and hiring new assistant professors, I think the following advice will be helpful for you.

WHAT KIND OF POSITION DO YOU WANT?

What kind of position do you want and in what kind of institution? The answers to these questions, which place your end goal in the forefront, should be related to what you want to be able to do as a result of gaining your doctorate, besides being a professor. For example, are you most interested in teaching or in research? You may not have an answer to this at first, but it is a question that you should continue to ask yourself. The answer will help you understand the type of institution you want to work with.

There are many kinds of institutions—public, private, research extensive, teaching focused, masters granting, liberal arts—and not all have the same emphasis when it comes to teaching, research, and service. The institutions that I am most familiar with are called research extensive institutions (sometimes called a Research I). In these institutions, tenure and promotion are strongly tied to your research productivity, grant activity, and publication record.

If this sounds appealing, and you consider research and writing as strengths, then you should consider aspiring to work in a research extensive or intensive institution. Having a desire to emphasize research and writing does not mean that you cannot place a high value on teaching as well. In fact, many research institutions do; rather, it means that you must be committed to and have strong skills in research and publishing.

If you determine that teaching and working with students are your greatest strengths, and that you are less interested in research and publication, then you should consider an institution that considers teaching to be most important. The majority of 4-year institutions as well as community colleges, which together amount to the largest sources of faculty employment, consider teaching as most important to their mission.

It is important to identify the content area in which you want to work. For example, if you would like to work in teacher education, then you will have the most success in achieving that goal if you do your doctoral work within a department or program focused on teacher education. I have known students whose goals did not match their areas of expertise, but I have never known any who successfully achieved their goals without first ensuring their goals were aligned with their expertise.

It is important to consider that, in a number of fields, jobs are less plentiful than in others. For example, in blended departments like educational leadership and policy, which is the type of department with which I am most familiar, educational policy positions are currently much less plentiful than educational leadership positions. It is important to make decisions about the field you are entering knowing the market for Ph.D.s.

Although supply and demand tend to fluctuate, you can gain a fairly strong understanding of the market by talking with your advisor and faculty from other programs and by scanning job postings in sources like the *Chronicle of Higher Education*, University Council for Educational Administration's (UCEA) online academic job site, and other online sources like *Inside Higher Education*.

FIND OUT HOW TO PREPARE

Once you know what kind of institution you want to become part of, you then need to understand what they would be looking for in candidates for assistant professor positions. Although position descriptions can be helpful, the best source of data can come from faculty members, particularly those who have participated on search committees for assistant professor positions within the past few years. You want to talk to them about the criteria they use to screen applicants, what makes some candidates more desirable than others, and what expectations they have for the candidates' experience with research, teaching, and service.

Once you know in which type of place you want to work and what the expectations are for new faculty in such institutions, you need to develop the knowledge, expertise, and experiences that will make you a viable candidate. As you begin to develop in these areas, you will want to record your achievements in what is called a curriculum vita, which is essentially an academic résumé.

It is important to begin developing your vita early, even though you will not necessarily have a great deal to put into it. One reason that it is helpful to start early is so that you can identify all of the areas that you will need to address as a scholar, such as publications, scholarly presentations, awards, teaching, and service. By the end of your doctoral program, you should aspire to have something listed under each of these categories.

Be careful not to make your vita too long, especially if you have never held an academic position. The faculty reviewing your vita will really only want to know about the experiences and achievements that you have accomplished that are related to the position you are seeking. Thus, you do not need to include a thorough description of every job you have ever held.

Your vita should accurately portray your skills and achievements, and how it is structured matters. In the UCEA online job search handbook, you will find helpful advice on developing a vita (among other resources for the job search). Take a look at this resource and other online sources as you develop your vita. You should ask your mentors for copies of their vitae, so that you can see how they categorize different forms of scholarly contributions. Furthermore, after you have put your vita together, ask your mentors to look it over and give you feedback.

THE IMPORTANCE OF RELATIONSHIPS

I cannot overestimate the importance of a mentor in higher education. Mentors are important to academics at every stage of their careers, and they are extremely important at the graduate student stage. Your first mentor may or may not be your advisor. What you want to do is find a mentor who will support you and who believes that by supporting you he or she benefits as well.

Usually these kinds of people have reputations for being good mentors and have successfully supported a number of young scholars before you came along. Once you have such a mentor, treat him or her well. Any time that they are spending on you and your career is time that they are not spending on other students or on themselves and their careers. Respect and appreciate their time and assistance.

Your mentors, advisors, faculty at your institution, and others from professional relationships will be the people who will serve as your job references. Your references do not need to be famous; however, they should be respected scholars from institutions similar to the ones for which you are applying. When contacting a reference, (a) explain what you would like them to do, (b) list your goals, (c) provide all information: description of the fellowship or position, a copy of your vita, and a copy of your letter of application. If they agree to serve as a reference, be sure to thank them by sending a thank you note or email.

When you are working on your degree, you are not the only graduate student in your program. Remember that those other graduate students are likely to be your career-long colleagues. Although you may not see eye to eye on certain issues, find the same areas captivating, or plan on ever collaborating, you should maintain professional, respectful relationships with them. Some doctoral students consider their peers to be competitors, and although in certain cases you may be competing with your peers for an award or fellowship, try to keep your open competitiveness to a minimum. Your colleagues may find your competitiveness to be wearing or distasteful, and you never know what kind of role they may play in your career.

THINGS YOU SHOULD BE DOING

In addition to developing your area of expertise, there are several key things you should be doing while you are in your doctoral program. One is that you should attend and at some point present at academic conferences. In addition to the opportunities to hear presentations, to learn about new lines of research, and to gain experience presenting, academic conferences are important places to develop your professional network.

Scholars who work in your area of expertise and related fields, including those whose work you have been reading or who you have seen referenced, will be conveniently gathered in one place for several days. Moreover, they are there to share and talk about their research and learn what others are doing and thinking about. Taken as a group, these are the scholars who are shaping your field, and you should engage with them. However, be aware, the quality of your encounters always matters. You want them to see you as a bright young scholar.

There are several ways to engage. One way is to attend sessions where the people you would like to meet are presenting their work. This kind of situation provides an opportunity for you to hear more about what they are working on, ask questions, and depending on the nature and size of the session, introduce yourself at the end of the session and have a brief conversation.

At times, presenters or discussions will extend beyond the session slot, making a more than hurried word of appreciation and introduction difficult. It is still worth your effort, because it can be built on in other venues, such as receptions. Receptions are good opportunities for networking and meeting new people. When you are new to the field, it is helpful to attend such events with your advisor or mentor so that they can make introductions.

A second thing you should do while working on your doctorate is develop your writing skills. Your first few attempts at writing as a doctoral student may be incredibly painful, either the process itself or reading the feedback from your professors. If you experience this, know that you are not alone. Many people struggle with writing.

One of my mentors, who helped me improve my writing immensely through amazingly close and patient editorial feedback, gave me some really good advice toward the beginning of my program. He suggested that I read William Zinsser's book *On Writing Well*. I had so much reading already that I almost didn't take his suggestion, but I am glad that I did. Zinsser provides a lot of useful advice on writing, the most important for me was to read! Read articles in the journals where you eventually intend to publish, identify articles that you really like, not just because of the content but also the way the author presented it.

If you find writers that you really admire, figure out why, and try some of the strategies they have used. How do they introduce their topic? How do they discuss their findings? What is the structure of their discussion? How do they transition between sections? You can learn a lot by reading good writing.

As your writing skills improve and you write more papers, you will want to submit some for publication. Think carefully about where to send your papers. Make sure the focus, methods, and length make the piece a good fit for the journal. Consider the journal's reputation concerning editorial feedback, timely reviews, and its acceptance rate. Even if your paper is rejected, you should receive helpful feedback that you can use to improve the paper before you submit it to a different journal. Having a paper accepted for publication while in graduate school is a wonderful achievement, and it will signal that you have the potential to be successful scholar.

Teaching is a third skill you should seek to develop during your doctoral program. Teaching is an important part of being a professor, and it does not come naturally for everyone. It is always a good idea to acquire a teaching assistantship during your program. In some institutions, you may even find a paid assistantship. However, even if you cannot find a paid position, it is a good idea to work with a professor to help deliver a course.

In some cases, you will have an opportunity to help a faculty member redesign his or her course, update the syllabus, and choose new readings. You will want to take any opportunity offered to help plan and teach classes during the semester. Ask the faculty member you are working with for these opportunities if they are not offered, and if they are offered, take them and request feedback on your performance. These experiences will help you (a) develop your skills in teaching adult learners, (b) teach a course in preparation for your first faculty position, and (c) provide a substantial experience to include on your vita.

More and more universities and professional associations are offering programs, usually seminars, focused on preparing graduate students for faculty positions. If your institution offers such a program, you should enroll. The interdisciplinary nature of university-wide programs offers a perspective on university culture that should be useful, and you are likely to leave the program with important information and helpful tips.

Professional associations like University Council For Educational Administration (UCEA) and American Educational Research Association (AERA), also offer sessions, workshops, and symposia focused on preparing graduate students for faculty positions. I highly recommend these as well. These seminars sometimes focus on teaching, sometimes on research, and sometimes on issues of concern to new faculty members like maintaining balance in your personal and professional life or grant writing.

PROCRASTINATION

There are many pitfalls on the way to obtaining your degree and a job in higher education. Procrastination is a major pitfall. I have seen it wreck academic careers. The never-ending editing or the analysis of a data set over and over just to see if something else might be at play are excuses for not finishing a project. In your graduate program, procrastination can occur at any point; it is most likely to occur when you are finished with your coursework and you have transitioned into the less-structured period of candidacy—working on your dissertation.

Several strategies for avoiding procrastinating include creating timelines for your work with benchmark goals, maintaining a standing appointment with your dissertation chair, and meeting with a support group of colleagues who are working on their dissertations to share progress, concerns, and strategies.

FINAL WORDS

Your choice to enter the professoriate brings with it the promise of a rich and stimulating career; it also brings with it a great deal of responsibility. Take your preparation seriously, and don't rush through it. Learning about the field, and becoming a part of it, is important, but remember that they are secondary to developing expertise in your area of specialization. Read broadly and deeply discuss, write, and reflect.

There is no better time to overindulge in these activities than when you are a doctoral student. Although you don't want to be a student forever, try to get as much out of every interaction and every experience as you possibly can. You really can afford to take your time.

REFERENCES

Chronicle of Higher Education. Retrieved March 15, 2010, http://chronicle.com/section/Jobs/61/

Inside Higher Education. Retrieved March 15, 2010, http://www.insidehighered.com/

University Council for Educational Administration (UCEA). Job search page. Retrieved March 15, 2010, www.ucea.org/edleadershipjobs/

University Council for Educational Administration (UCEA). Job search handbook. Retrieved March 15, 2010, http://www.ucea.org/job-search-handbook/

Zinsser, W. (2006). *On writing well: The classic guide to writing nonfiction* (New York: HarperCollins).

20

Using the Dissertation as a Vehicle for Publishing: A Conversation Between Professor and Doctoral Student

Dr. Charles L. Slater
California State University–Long Beach

Mtra. Gema López Gorosave
Escuela Normal Estatal in Ensenada, B.C., México

Gema López Gorosave is a doctoral student at the Universidad Autónoma de Baja (UABC) California, and Charles Slater is her dissertation advisor, as well as professor at California State University Long Beach (CSULB). Following the signing of an agreement between CSULB and UABC, Gema came to CSULB as a scholar in residence for the spring semester 2009. She attended classes and met with professors including Dr. Xin Li, an expert in narrative inquiry. Dr. Li begins her work with students by discussing their personal history and motives for study (Li, 2002). I became convinced of the importance of understanding students in this way and began a discussion with Gema.

There are many important questions about presenting and publishing that we will not address in this chapter. Students need to know about professional organizations and journals in their area. They need to understand the format of academic writing and how to go about conducting a literature review and framing a question. These issues are best studied in many of the research texts in the field such as Calabrese (2006), Creswell (2003), Glatthorn and Joyner (2005), Merriam and Simpson (2000), and Piantanida and Garman (2009).

Too often, advice on dissertation topics, presentations, and publications is based on the professor's interest without attention to the life of the student. Even worse, writing for publication is sometimes viewed as a purely technical process or an obstacle to be overcome on the way to earning a degree. This approach is an attempt to listen to the student and understand her important life experiences.

Once there is greater understanding of the context in which a student studies, teaches, and writes, the answers to questions about publishing flow more freely. The first goal is to write from the heart; the second is to express the truth, and only then to submit for publication.

Gema and I attempted to address these profound issues with a few simple questions. The intent was to encourage Gema to tell her story first so I could give direction to her scholarly work. We started with her childhood and continued through her career to her current challenges. Through Gema's story, and the process of telling her story, she and I were able to think through the experiences that shaped who she was and then incorporate these past experiences as a starting point for her academic pursuits, including not only writing the dissertation but also in framing a long-term research agenda.

Dr. Slater: Tell me about your childhood and how you grew up?

Gema: I was born while my father and his collaborators were planning the first normal school as the apex of what was then the new state educational system in Baja California. They were always talking about the challenges of education. It was a bohemian atmosphere with a guitar and boleros that played into the night. I used to stay awake to listen to them.

I remember seeing my father on television. They interviewed him frequently and praised his eloquence. He was an excellent orator, presenter, and professor.

Dr. Slater: Where did your father grow up?

Gema: My father was young when his father died, and his mother moved the family to San Luciano, a small mining town in Baja California Sur, where she became the town's teacher. When my father grew up, he became a union activist and led mining strikes in Santa Rosalia. Because of his activities, he had to flee to the next state to the north, Baja California. He carried a letter of recommendation from one of his teachers that introduced him to the governor. He was so impressed that he asked him to establish a school system and named him the first supervisor of education.

Dr. Slater: What was your father's philosophy of education?

Gema: My father promoted arts, culture, sports, and education. He said that students and teachers should have a broad experience through reading and sports. He used to emphasize the importance of sports by pointing to an Olympic runner, Queta Basilio, who was discovered when he won Olympic trials in rural areas.

He was a daring leader. As president of the municipal basketball league, he attended a national meeting when they were going to decide the site for the national basketball tournament and convention of delegates. He argued for Ensenada even though there was no facility. He was successful in having Ensenada named as host. When he returned, he had to convince the town of the necessity of building a gymnasium to hold the event. He thought that an event of this magnitude would motivate young people in sports. Ultimately, they built what is today the municipal gymnasium.

Dr. Slater: Did your father like his work?

Gema: He was happy working. He visited schools that he had founded across the length and breadth of the state. He wrote an editorial column in the newspaper that was the most well read in the area. He wrote political analysis, opinion, poetry, and essays.

I remember one column in which he made an emotional appeal for land to build the normal school and several sports fields. Abelardo L. Rodriguez, the ex-president of Mexico, lived in Ensenada. He was persuaded to give up his own land for the school.

I liked to listen to my father speak of teachers in his charge. He described them as people of broad culture that served as a model for the people. He told us that all he has become was due to his teachers. He was a product of the system of rural Mexican schools founded by General Lázaro Cárdenas in the 1940s.

Dr. Slater: Your father was a giant of a man. Did he have personal qualities that you particularly admired?

Gema: He was a hard and strong man on the outside, but on the inside, he was extremely sensitive, an artist and singer who played the piano and guitar. He was the life of the party, but he took refuge in reading, especially poetry.

My father assisted anyone in need. Often I would answer a knock on the door of our house and see a poor person from the countryside who offered a humble gift for my father, such as a box of tomatoes, an onion he had raised, or a fish. Usually the message was like this, "Tell the professor that I, Juan Perez, have not forgotten the favor that he did for me five years ago.

Dr. Slater: Have you seen this kind of gratitude in your life?

Gema: I remember the first day that I met with the directors that I invited to be part of my dissertation study. One of the most timid of them approached me and said, "I want you to know that I have come to participate because you are the daughter of the professor who helped me enter the normal school."

Dr. Slater: It seems that you had a happy childhood with your father. Were there any negative experiences?

Gema: My father wanted us to be aware of suffering and poverty, and he showed us difficult places such as jails that housed children. He wanted to release those who had committed small crimes. On one Mother's Day, he was able to arrange the release of a child and looked forward to seeing the joy of the mother and child reunited. But the mother did not want to see the child. We were so sad. My father was angry against the forces that created such misery.

I remember a day when I opened the door to find a woman who had a baby in her arms. She asked for help because the baby she carried was her son who had died. My father took the woman and her son to the Red Cross. When he returned, we wondered why the baby had died, and he told us that it had happened because of poverty that is always accompanied by ignorance.

Dr. Slater: You have spoken admiringly of your father. Did he have a great influence over your choice of career and pursuit of a dissertation?

Gema: I am the only teacher of seven siblings. I always wanted to follow this career despite my elementary teachers who told me that I was intelligent and should not be a teacher. I never doubted it. My grandmother wanted my father to send me to study in the most famous normal school in Mexico City. But he said that I should study in the normal school that he had founded.

I was excited to enter the normal school of my dreams, but it was not long before I learned that the school was not the one I had dreamed about. It did not seem like a good school. I was bored. The dream was broken.

When I studied at the normal school, there was no requirement to graduate from high school. You could enter directly from middle school. I started at age 14, and I was bored in my classes, they sapped my energy, and the school did not offer me what I had hoped for. My expectations were too high. I had a particular image of a professor that I would encounter, but it was not fulfilled.

One day, a professor who was the director of a rural school told us that he did not have a teacher for fourth grade and wondered if someone could cover the class as a practicum without pay. No one responded. I went home and told my parents that I wanted to cover the class because I was wasting my time at the normal school. They approved, and the next day I began. I knew absolutely nothing about teaching classes to 12-year-old students.

Dr. Slater: When did you start teaching in a regular position?

Gema: The government had no money to hire teachers. They needed many teachers and young people like me who were able to give classes because they did not pay us. Neither did they pay the normal school teachers because we were in difficult times. I occupied my time in service, but I did not abandon the idea of being a teacher. I looked for opportunities to study, but there were not many. When they opened, I took them.

I received a full-time teaching appointment in a primary school and almost immediately, the normal school invited me to fill a position. At the same time, I studied for a bachelor's degree. During the school year, I worked each day in the primary school in the morning, two days in the middle school in the afternoon, three afternoons in the normal school, and three evenings in the high school.

When I finished my bachelor's, I started working at la Universidad Pedagógica Nacional (UPN-Ensenada). At the age of 28, I left all of these positions to teach at the normal school and raise my two sons. I joined the first cohort in a master's degree at UPN-Tijuana. My mother, my father, and my husband all became ill during this time, and I cared for them until they died.

Dr. Slater: I am sorry that your husband died at a young age. You continued teaching for many years at the normal school. When did you become director?

Gema: I never thought I would be the director of the normal school. I was happy teaching but was not interested in administration. I was always a teacher who sought to innovate. I had confidence in myself. They asked me to take over the direction of the school. It was not what I desired most, but I felt that I had a moral obligation to fulfill. I am proud of my work there, but the school has still not achieved the ideal. There is much work left to do.

Dr. Slater: Why did you decide to pursue a doctorate?

Gema: Since 1997, I have been involved in regional and national reform efforts. I met many highly educated professors from other schools with distinct visions for normal schools. For me a university education was a necessity. My master's thesis was a study of teacher evaluation. My professor, Dr. Edna Luna, invited me to participate in an interinstitutional research study of teaching. I wanted to pursue more opportunities than other professors at the normal school who were content with their current level of education. I was well aware that many of my friends had enrolled in national and international doctoral courses, and my three brothers had studied medicine outside of the state.

Dr. Slater: Why did you select leadership practices of school directors as your dissertation topic?

Gema: My first passion was mathematics, but the only career opportunities were in teacher education. I continued my master's work on teacher formation, and this is the area I would have chosen. About 8 years ago, I joined a group of universities that were organizing the design of a new teacher preparation program. I asked for a sabbatical to work on the development of a postgraduate program as part of a national reform of normal schools.

I wanted to work in the area of mathematics or Spanish, but there were not enough people interested in these areas. I chose the third area: reform of educational management. Dr. Jose Maria Garcia and scholars at UABC designed the program, and I became the coordinator of the postgraduate program at the normal school. I worked with Dr. Garcia to undertake a research study on educational administration in postgraduate education, and he urged me to pursue a doctorate.

Dr. Slater: I met you when I was conducting focus groups of school directors at UABC in October, 2004. You expressed interest in our study, which eventually became part of a 13-nation collaboration, the International Study of Principal Preparation (ISPP).

Gema: Yes, I began my own research study in 2007 and was accepted to the doctoral program Instituto de Investigación y Desarrollo Educativo at UABC. I asked you to be my doctoral advisor and for Dr. Jose Maria Garcia to serve on the dissertation committee. We began to make presentations (Garcia, Gorosave, & Slater, 2007; Slater, Garcia, & Gorosave, 2007a, 2007b, 2007c, 2008b) and completed a publication in the *Journal of Educational Administration* (Slater, Garcia, & Gorosave, 2008a). I even traveled to Calgary, Alberta, Canada, to participate in an ISPP meeting.

Dr. Slater: I think it was important that you joined our research team to make presentations and write for publication. The doctoral program requires you to be the first author of two professional presentations and an article in a refereed journal. These are major undertakings.

Gema: They do not frighten me. I have already covered the requirement to make two presentations. The first was Santiago, Chile (Gorosave, Garcia, & Slater, 2007) and the second in Veracruz, Mexico (Gorosave, Garcia, & Slater, 2009).

I have not done anything to complete an article. The results from the first round of data collection would make a good article. I have started to validate the categories, but the program deadline to finish the article is only 5 months away. What would you think of an article about principals' styles of leadership in their first year in the journal *Psicoperspectivas*?

The problem is that I have to present at the colloquium at the end of the month, and then there is a progress meeting with the thesis committee the following month. In addition, if I return to teaching, it will put me behind.

Dr. Slater: Let's take one step at a time. First, you have prepared wisely for the colloquium by spending most of your time on the third chapter, the methods. You can return to the literature review in the second chapter later. Second, the time between the colloquium and the progress meeting with the thesis committee is tight, but you will get specific critiques of your chapters. Focus on these critiques and do what you can before the meeting. Third, I endorse your approach of taking the material from your initial results to put together the required article. The colloquium and the thesis meeting should both contribute to what you will write.

One of the themes in your personal narrative is the perseverance to work through difficult situations and the persistence to return to important endeavors in your life. This strength of character will serve you well in the year ahead. I also see a lifelong commitment to the normal school of Ensenada and normal schools throughout Mexico.

Take just a moment to look ahead to the time when you complete your dissertation. What will you want to accomplish?

Gema: With the second data collection, I will write one or perhaps two articles for publication. I enjoy the process of research. It is quite different from teaching, an area where I was comfortable. I want to commit myself to research in practice and maintain contact with teachers and elementary school directors. Research requires time, a budget, and networks of researchers. If I returned to teaching at the normal school, it would be difficult for me to develop as a researcher because the school environment is not conducive to research, and I risk having my doctorate appear inconsequential.

I would become an impressive statistic: the first doctoral graduate from the normal school of Ensenada, nothing more. If on the other hand, my retirement grants me the right, I would have many more possibilities to develop as a researcher. I would always like to be in a network and participate with Ibero-American researchers. The interchange of ideas has provided new perspectives.

The normal school has given much to me and has formed me as a teacher. It has been my pleasure to teach, earn a good salary, have economic security, and a quality of life, but it has limited my development as a professional. I have always had to open other spaces to satisfy my need to know more, to break the routine, and not to conform to the exigencies of the daily life of teaching.

REFERENCES

Calabrese, R. (2006). *The elements of an effective dissertation and thesis: A step by step guide for getting it right the first time.* Lanham, MD: Rowman & Littlefield.

Creswell, J. W. (2003). Research design: Qualitative, quantitative, and mixed methods approaches. Thousand Oaks, CA: Sage.

Garcia, J. M., Gorosave, G., & Slater, C. L. (2007, November). El Director de Escuela Primaria en su Primer Año de Servicio: Un estudio de la Carga Administrativa que Enfrenta. Congreso Nacional de Investigación Educativa, Merida, Mexico.

Glatthorn, A., & Joyner, R. (2005). *Writing the winning thesis or dissertation: A step-by-step guide.* Thousand Oaks, CA: Corwin.

Gorosave, G. L., Garcia, J. M., & Slater, C. L. (2007). Como resuelven los problemas los directores eficaces? Un estudio de directores de primaria mexicanos en su primer ano de servicio. *Revista Electronica Iberoamericana sobre Calidad, Eficacia, y Cambio en Educacion,* 5(5e), 139–143.

Gorosave, G. L., Garcia, J. M., & Slater, C. L. (2009). Las prácticas de dirección y liderazgo en las escuelas, primarias públicas: El caso de Rebeca. Congreso Nacional de Investigación Educativa, Veracruz, Mexico.

Li, X. (2002). *The Tao of life stories: Chinese language, poetry, and culture in education.* New York: Peter Lang.

Merriam, S. B., & Simpson, E. L. (2000). *A guide to research for educators and trainers of adults.* Malabar, FL: Drieger.

Piantanida, M., & Garman, N. B. (2009). *The qualitative dissertation: A guide for students and faculty.* Thousand Oaks, CA: Corwin.

Slater, C. L., Garcia, J. M., & Gorosave, G. (2007a, April). The authority of the new principal. American Educational Research Association Conference, Chicago, IL.

Slater, C. L., Garcia, J. M., & Lopez Gorosave, G. (2007b, September). The challenges of a successful first-year principal in Mexico: The devil is in the paperwork. European Educational Research Association, Ghent, Belgium.

Slater, C. L., Garcia, J. M., & Gorosave, G. L. (2007c, November). The challenges of a successful first-year principal in Mexico: Structural, human resource, symbolic, and political perspectives. Paper presented at the University Council for Educational Administration, Alexandria, VA.

Slater, C. L., Garcia, J. M., & Gorosave, G. (2008a). Challenges of a successful first-year principal in Mexico. *Journal of Educational Administration, 46*(6), 702–714.

Slater, C. L., Garcia, J. M., & Gorosave, G. (2008b, July). Challenges of diversity faced by Mexican school directors. Paper presented at the British Educational Leadership, Management, and Administration Society Conference, Birmingham, England.

21

Maximizing Your Dissertation to Propel Your Career

Dr. George Theoharis
Syracuse University

I benefited from sage advice both through the dissertation process and as my career as a scholar began. Much of that advice directly relates to being strategic to maximize my dissertation to propel my early career as an academic. In an effort to be transparent about the advice and lessons I learned, this chapter provides key strategies I was given and used successfully. I recognize that not all of my advice will work for you, and that aspects of these ideas will be more applicable to some than to others.

TOPIC MATTERS

First and perhaps most importantly, choose the topic of the dissertation with care. I was told, "this is way too much work for it not to matter to you and to others." This concept should not paralyze you into feeling the need to pick the flashiest or engaging area. I know when I am passionate about a topic or question, I work harder, longer, and the work sustains me.

I recognize that many people complete their dissertation by working on a larger faculty-initiated project, and that can be fine, but be sure to consider two criteria in your topic selection: (a) What are the issues that you keep coming back to in your work and your thinking? I call this the "what keeps you up at night" test; and (b) what about that topic is of keen interest to others? I call this the "why would anyone else care about this" test.

For example, I worked with a doctoral student who did project after project about parent involvement and the relationship between mothers and schools. Yet, what she really cared about most was a play and language-based kindergarten and early childhood program. When she switched her topic to what she cared about more, her motivation increased and the work progressed much more quickly.

FRAMING THE STUDY, RESEARCH QUESTIONS, AND BEING STRATEGIC

Defining the research questions and guiding the purpose of the study need to be done with great care and consultation. Use two to three well-crafted research questions. Although this is fairly typical advice, seeing two to three distinct aspects of the topic and how they come together will allow for this work to live on past graduation. Some of the best advice I was given is to use the data addressing each of these questions to create stand-alone articles.

Along with the importance of crafting research questions that can be used for publishable work is the importance of having one aspect or strand of your literature review be comprehensive. You need to know everything (or almost everything) written on that aspect or strand. This should be something closely related to your emerging research questions. This knowledge is important to construct a quality dissertation and make you a better scholar. You can also publish a synthesis or review on that aspect of the literature as a stand-alone article.

After your dissertation is defended be strategic and map out how you can maximize distinct articles and even a book from your work. Ask others including your mentors and colleagues to assist you in this strategic process. Try to (a) publish a piece in the premier journal in your specific field, (b) publish other articles for other important journals in your field, (c) create a manuscript that would have broad appeal outside of your specific field in a premier journal, (d) look for refereed journals interested in specific frameworks or lens, or (e) create a synthesis or literature review article.

When outlining the articles you might generate from your research questions, think about the following issues. What aspect of these questions would appeal to a broader audience? What aspect has a specific audience; can you craft a piece for that group? What different frameworks or methodologies can you apply to create different manuscripts? For example, one manuscript I wrote relied on autoethographic narrative to guide the structure and themes. Another relied on an activist research framework and only used the voices or words of the participants I studied to tell their stories and explain the way they framed their experiences.

OTHER WAYS OF PROMOTING YOUR DISSERTATION

As you craft manuscripts from your dissertation, be attentive to what other themes or materials you have in your data that you could revisit, expand upon, further investigate, or on which to complete a secondary analysis. For me, this meant a theme that did not relate to my research questions but was constructed in the discussion of my dissertation. I looked specifically at part of the data to address new research questions. Being mindful of these possibilities will allow you to create additional stand-alone manuscripts.

Two additional pieces of advice were to present your work widely and apply for dissertation awards. Take aspects of your work and present your work at multiple conferences. Dissertation awards are an opportunity for people who do not know your work to read it and use it. I suggest talking to your mentors and colleagues about this. Say "this professor (feel free to use my name) suggested I apply for a dissertation award. Which award would be appropriate for me?" Winning an award positions your work to be both more widely known and valued. I know a number of faculty members who have served on dissertation award committees who shared dissertation work of nonwinners (with permission) with others doing similar work, which resulted positively for the nonwinner.

This chapter provides various ways for you to maximize your dissertation to help successfully propel you into academia. Clearly, your topic is of great importance. If you intend to use these strategies, remember the work on your topic during the dissertation process to completion will extend for years afterward. So, you better love it.

These strategies allowed me to move successfully into higher education. I am indebted to those who provided me with this advice that I shared with you. Most of this advice came from my mentor Colleen Capper. Yet Madeline Hafner, John Rogers, Kathleen Brown, Linda Skrla, Mary Louise Gomez, Michael Apple, Paul Bredeson, Clif Conrad, Gerardo Lopez, Sari Biklen, Flo Hamrick, and Kelly Chandler-Olcott have provided important guidance that shaped this chapter's content.

I took their advice and now pay it forward. As an emerging scholar, I wrote an overview of my dissertation for the premier journal in educational leadership [Theoharis, G. (2007). Social justice educational leaders and resistance: Toward a theory of social justice leadership. *Educational Administration Quarterly, 43*(2), 221–258]. I wrote a synthesis of an aspect of my literature [Theoharis, G. (2007). Navigating rough waters: A synthesis of the countervailing pressures against leading for social justice. *Journal of School Leadership, 17*(1), 4–27].

I broke up my research questions and created three manuscripts [Theoharis, G. (in press). Disrupting injustice: Strategies public school principals use to advance social justice. *Teachers College Record*; Theoharis, G. (in press). Sustaining social justice: Strategies urban principals develop to advance justice and equity while facing resistance. *International Journal of Urban Educational Leadership*; and Theoharis, G. (2008). "At every turn": The resistance public school principals face in their pursuit of equity and justice. *Journal of School Leadership, 18*(3), 303–343].

I reframed the entire study for a book published by Teachers College Press [Theoharis, G. (2009). *The leadership our children deserve: 7 keys to equity, social justice, and school reform.* New York: Teachers College Press].

I also produced other works [Theoharis, G. (in press). "Yes we can": Social justice principals navigate resistance to create equitable and excellent schools. In S. Horsford (Ed.), *New perspectives in educational leadership: Exploring social, political, and community contexts and meaning.* New York: Peter Lang; Theoharis, G. (2008). Woven in deeply: Identity and leadership of urban social justice principals. *Education and Urban Society, 41*(1), 3–25; Dotger, B., & Theoharis, G. (2008). From disposition to action: Bridging moral/ethical reasoning and social justice leadership. *Values and Ethics in Educational Administration, 6*(3), 1–8; Theoharis, G. (2009, April). Raising student achievement: Toward a theory of socially just school reform. Paper presented at American Education Research Association Annual Meeting, San Diego, CA].

22

What Do You Want to Do With This? Means-Driven Dissertation Writing

Dr. Catherine Lugg
Rutgers, State University of New Jersey

Many doctoral students find themselves at a loss when developing a research topic, much less considering their professional lives after they've completed the dissertation. While they can easily envision the much anticipated return to a normal life once the dissertation is complete, successfully defended, and they have become a "Doctor," they're less sure about whether their exhaustive (and exhausting) efforts have resulted only in a mere hefty and expensive doorstop.

Consequently, before they even get to the dissertation stage, I encourage my doctoral students to consider what they want to "do" with their dissertations. Yes, each and every dissertation is going to expand the research base, because that is the point of the entire venture. But that lofty goal generally isn't substantive enough to get, much less keep, most doctoral students focused. So I try to get my doctoral students to think in more concrete terms.

If they're planning on being a professor, I encourage them to "own" an area of research. Quite simply, if they can't command the research literature on their topic, they're not ready to begin their dissertation. Why I'm so insistent on this point is that this area and the supporting research areas will generate not only their dissertation, but their research agenda for the next 10 years.

The transition from graduate student to professor is filled with multiple distractions. It generally entails moving, setting up multiple offices (one at home and at work), securing a new research site or sites (or finding important local and state archives), as well as negotiating through multiple bureaucracies, from the new-to-you university, to the cable company, to the department of motor vehicles (my least favorite task). It can mean moving one's partner (and his or her job), children (and their schools), and possibly significant elders.

If a new faculty member doesn't have a lot of material already at his or her fingertips, once the dissertation is turned into publication, there is a noticeable lag in subsequent research publications. And that time lag can become a time bomb when one is working against the tenure time clock.

For those doctoral students who wish to remain in the field as an administrator or teacher, I encourage them to own an area or areas that will help them in their job—both now and in the future. With the "research-based reform" mandate of No Child Left Behind (NCLB), working teachers and administrators need to command the research literature for a different reason: snake oil avoidance.

Many prepackaged curriculum pushers—*publishers*—tout the research base of their wares, only noting in the teeny-tiny print that the research foundation in question is a market research, not a true evaluation of their product(s). Additionally, a number of doctoral students have envisioned becoming consults to districts and educational organizations postgraduation. Commanding the research base in their areas brings greater credibility and competitive advantage in an era of endless, frontal-lobe depleting, "drive-by" professional workshops offered by credentialed hucksters.

Most importantly, both sets of students need to pick a research area that they can obsess about, love, and freely inflict on their families and friends. The traditional model of dissertation advising involves a faculty member securing doctoral students to work with them on the faculty member's research agenda.

In my own case, that has been highly improbable since my major two research areas can be considered "high cootie factor" topics: The Protestant right and their involvement in U.S. educational politics; and the queer rights movements and politics of public schooling in the United States and Canada. Both topics have not been big draws for doctoral students in educational administration/policy—or grant funding agencies for that matter. Yet I teach in an area (educational administration) that historically has served a large number of doctoral students. So I will always be coaching a fair number of dissertations if I am to meet my obligations to my colleagues (i.e., share the load of dissertation advising).

Consequently, my dissertation students know upfront that they need to claim an area that interests them and, if need be, they need to seek their own funding if they wish to have their work grant funded. They need to pick their dissertation committee members fairly carefully so they can gain the supportive expertise they need to complete their dissertations.

As the academe-bound doctoral students move through their coursework, projects, and into dissertations, they are generally presenting their research at conferences. They get experience testing out possible topics, as well as gain practice presenting in scholarly venues.

They are also introduced to the time pressures of getting the initial proposal submitted to the conference's sponsor (generally, University Council for Educational Administration [UCEA], HES, and AERA), as well as completing a paper in the midst of the academic term—while they are teaching (as teaching assistants). The doctoral students who wish to remain in their professional fields generally do not present at academic conferences before they defend their dissertations, but have done so when their busy schedules permit.

Along the way, I encourage my students to have family and friends critically read their work. I have done this myself since I was a doctoral student, and sometimes it's our family members who can give us the most honest assessment of our work.

In several cases I have helped students turn their dissertations into publications, serving as a friendly but skeptical critic or coauthor. In other instances, I have helped them incorporate some of the findings into new articles and book chapters that cover related topics. Perhaps for the vast majority of both groups of doctoral students, however, the best virtue of this approach is their research is truly their own. For these new colleagues in venues where researcher independence is critical (like academe, but also in some superintendencies), they have already demonstrated that they truly are "their own professional."

For all of the upsides to this approach, there are a few downsides. First, while I am most happy to coach eager students, if the student in question wants to conduct a dissertation using hierarchical linear modeling (HLM), I should not and will not chair. Similarly, if their dissertation is fairly innovative on the qualitative side, the dissertation student had best have a dedicated methodologist on their committee—or have someone else chair.

My methodological background is that of a traditional historian—my research subjects are quite dead or otherwise inaccessible. While I can help in both quantitative and qualitative studies by catching some basic design flaws, odd research questions, unvoiced assumptions and presumptions, if things get methodologically "weedy," I'm out of field. Similarly, this approach hinges on whether the individual student in question is strongly self-motivated and self-directed. This is not always the case with every student—whether they wish to remain in the field or aspire for a faculty position.

While this approach does not work for every doctoral student, I think for highly motivated students, it's been quite helpful. They've been able to focus both on the immediate task (the dissertation) and the longer-term task (what am I going to use this for?). And I've been fortunate to coach a wide range of dissertations, from the impact of the African American civil rights movement on the National Education Association, to how both normal and hearing disabled students construct culture in their mainstreamed elementary classroom, to how novice teachers learn the politics of their jobs (to name a few). Some of my former dissertation students have been able to use their dissertations as a "pivot," transitioning either into academe or into better positions in the field.

Final Thoughts

When we, as editors, first discussed the prospects of producing a book about mentoring and the doctoral process, our thoughts were directed to John Wooden, University of California–Los Angeles' (UCLA) legendary basketball coach. In the ever-changing and tumultuous world of sports, there is almost universal agreement that the "Wizard of Westwood" stands as the most successful coach in the history of college athletics. During his 27-year tenure with his beloved Bruins, Coach Wooden gained lasting fame with UCLA by accumulating a record winning streak of 88 games and four perfect 30–0 seasons. Under his direction, they won a record 98 straight home games at Pauley Pavilion and garnered 38 straight National Collegiate Athletic Association (NCAA) tournament wins.

Overall, Wooden's collegiate coaching career highlights 664 victories compared to only 162 losses for an astonishing 0.804 winning percentage. However, his 10 NCAA basketball titles during his last 12 seasons, including 7 in a row from 1967 to 1973, are commonly acknowledged as unique accomplishments that will stand the test of time. Notwithstanding his incredible coaching legacy, John Wooden is quick to point out that his "job" is that of a teacher, and that mentoring the "young men" that connect with him is his true calling.

American feminist and educational philosopher Nel Noddings's (1984) work on ethical caring parallels John Wooden's mentoring viewpoint. Like Wooden, Noddings approaches human interaction from the vantage of prioritizing relationships. She argues that the caregiving person (mentor) freely and willingly engrosses him- or herself through benefiting the person who receives the care (mentee).

In essence, authentic caring (mentorship) involves the mentor motivationally displacing him- or herself by prioritizing the needs of the person for whom he or she is caring (mentee). Nel Noddings refers to this concept as ethical caring, where a person's actions reflect a purposeful thoughtfulness about the appropriate way of relating to others. We, as editors of this book, simply call this great mentoring.

Our contributors share Coach Wooden's passion for teaching and Dr. Noddings' philosophy of ethical caring. Their doctoral students' success is important to them. It is academe's way of passing the baton from one generation to the next. Twenty-five major professors and dissertation advisors mentored you in this book. They offered you the same advice they would offer to one of their students. We encourage you to contact the contributors of this book with questions you might have about their mentoring advice. To that end, it has often been stated that experience is the best teacher. We are grateful for their contributions.

REFERENCES

Maxwell, J. C. (2001). *The 17 indisputable laws of teamwork: Embrace them and empower your team.* Nashville, TN: Thomas Nelson.

Noddings, N. (1984). *Caring: A feminine approach to ethics and moral education.* Berkeley: University of California Press.

Biographies

ABOUT THE EDITORS

Dr. Raymond L. Calabrese is professor of educational administration in the School of Educational Policy and Leadership at The Ohio State University. He is recognized as an academic scholar with a rich background across K–12 and higher education. His research focuses on appreciative inquiry—an action research methodology and change process focusing on identifying the best in people and their organizations. (Visit his appreciative inquiry blog at http://people.ehe.ohio-state.edu/rcalabrese/) He is the author of five books and coauthor of four books. His recent standalone books include *The Dissertation Desk Reference: The Doctoral Student's Manual to Writing the Dissertation*; *The Elements of an Effective Dissertation and Thesis: A Step by Step Guide for Getting it Right the First Time*; and *The Leadership Assignment: Creating Change*. His published work also includes over 100 refereed articles in educational journals such as the *Journal of School Leadership*, *Journal of Research on Leadership Education*, and the *Journal of Research for Educational Leaders*. He is also the principal investigator for several action research field study reports. He consistently presents his research at educational conferences such as the American Educational Research Association. He has received honors for his research, publications, and teaching. He earned his doctorate at the University of Massachusetts at Amherst. He can be contacted at calabrese.31@osu.edu

Dr. Page A. Smith is professor of educational leadership and policy studies at the University of Texas at San Antonio (UTSA). His research pursuits target organizational studies and involve quantitative analysis. Specifically, his scholarly areas of emphasis include organizational climate and health, institutional trust, collective efficacy, student aggression and bullying, and institutional change and influence. Accordingly, his most recent publications (*Educational Administration Quarterly*, *International Journal of Education Management*, *Journal of School Leadership*, and *Journal of Education Administration*) reflect his contributions to the field in these areas. He is currently conducting research in the areas of school culture, change orientation, and leadership influence. He pursues an active role in connecting theory to practice via graduate teaching forums, site consultations, professional development initiatives, and school-community liaison service. He serves as the associate dean for graduate studies in the College of Education and Human Development at UTSA. He can be contacted at Page.Smith@utsa.edu

ABOUT THE CONTRIBUTORS

Dr. Mary Frances Agnello is associate professor at Texas Tech University in Lubbock. She received her bachelor of arts degree from the University of Texas at Austin majoring in French, foreign language education, and government. After several years of teaching in Houston urban and Texas rural public high schools, she completed a master's and doctor of philosophy in curriculum and instruction at Texas A & M University in College Station, focusing her work in foundations of education and language, literacy, and culture. She spent 8 years in San Antonio at the University of Texas at San Antonio and at Our Lady of the Lake University working in teacher education, foundations, and educational leadership. Her research at Texas Tech University focuses on preservice teachers' knowledge in the social studies curriculum and critical pedagogy. She can be contacted at maryfrances.agnello@ttu.edu

Dr. Jeanne T. Amlund is assistant professor of educational psychology at the Pennsylvania State University, Greater Allegheny. She received her

Ph.D. in educational psychology from Arizona State University. Her research interests have included text processing and recall, study behaviors of college students, learning and computer technology in traditional and distance classrooms, and effects of beliefs and rereading on recall and comprehension. She was recognized for "excellence in academic advising" by the Commonwealth College of the Pennsylvania State University in 2003 and by the Pennsylvania State University in 2005. She can be contacted at jta@psu.edu

Dr. Pamela Angelle is assistant professor in educational leadership and policy studies where she mentors doctoral students at The University of Tennessee–Knoxville. Prior to her appointment to the professorate, she was a school improvement coordinator for the Louisiana Department of Education where she assisted PreK–12 schools in organizational change and improvement. Her research interests include school reform, with a focus on distributed leadership and those organizational conditions and contexts that contribute to a collegial school community. Recently, she has authored articles in the *Journal of School Leadership*, *Research in Middle Level Education*, and *Middle School Journal*. She can be contacted at pangelle@utk.edu

Dr. Rosemary S. Caffarella, professor of adult and extension education and international professor in education in the Department of Education at Cornell University, received her Ph.D. from Michigan State University. She has authored or coauthored seven books, and numerous book chapters and articles. She received the Cyril O. Houle World Award for Literature in Adult Education for the second and third editions of *Learning in Adulthood: A Comprehensive Guide* (1999, 2007), coauthored with Sharan Merriam and Lisa Baumgartner. She was honored through her initiation to the International Adult and Continuing Education Hall of Fame. Her ongoing major research and development project is a collaborative project on breast cancer education in Malaysia, with the major goal of building a sustainable program for and by Malaysians. She can be contacted at rsc29@cornell.edu

Dr. Patti L. Chance is professor and chair of the Department of Educational Leadership at San Diego State University. Her areas of interest and expertise include instructional leadership, supervision, school and curriculum improvement, and organizational behavior and leadership theory.

She is author or coauthor of three books, including her second edition of *An Introduction to Educational Leadership and Organizational Behavior: Theory into Practice*, an introductory text for educational administration, published in 2009. She has served as a journal editor of a national, refereed education journal and currently sits on editorial boards for several national journals devoted to educational leadership. Her published research is related to instructional supervision, educational administration preparation programs, rural schools, and leading for systemic change. She can be contacted at pchance@mail.sdsu.edu

Dr. Stacey Edmonson is professor and director of the Center for Research and Doctoral Studies in Educational Leadership at Sam Houston State University in Huntsville, Texas, where she teaches courses in qualitative research, school law, policy and ethics, and contemporary issues in education. Formerly she served as teacher, principal, and central office administrator in Texas public schools. Her scholarship agenda includes stress and burnout among educators, legal issues in education, and educator ethics. She has presented at several national and state conferences and has authored numerous journal articles and three books. She has held leadership positions in a number of educational leadership organizations, including the National Council of Professors of Educational Administration and the Southwest Education Research Association. She can be contacted at edu_sle01@shsu.edu

Dr. Connie L. Fulmer is associate professor in administrative leadership and policy studies (ALPS) in the School of Education and Human Development (SEHD) at the University of Colorado Denver (UCD). She and her colleagues deliver a principal-licensure program in partnership with Denver metro area school districts. She is currently serving in SEHD as chair of the program leaders. She was coauthor of the *Principal Accomplishments: How School Leaders Succeed*. She is working on a synthesis of leadership and coaching literature to develop a model of "Leading With a Coaching Mindset." The educational leadership programs at UCD were selected with seven other institutions for the UCEA-Wallace Leveraging Change Project. She co-chairs the Conference-Within-a-Conference (CWC) held in partnership with the National Council of Professors of Educational Administration (NCPEA) and three professional organizations, American Association of School Administrators (AASA), National Association of Secondary School Principals (NASSP), and the National Association of Elementary School Principals (NAESP). She can be contacted at Connie.Fulmer@ucdenver.edu

Dr. María Luisa González is associate dean of the College of Education at University of Texas at El Paso and Patricia Daw Yetter Professor. Formerly, she served at New Mexico State University for 21 years as faculty member, department head, and regents professor. She designed several doctoral programs for working educational leaders. She supported the successful completion of 25 doctoral dissertations. She served in various national organizations including the International Association for Supervision and Curriculum Development, the National Council for the Advancement of Teacher Education, and was president of the University Council of Educational Administration. She received several awards during her university career including the Dean's Service Award, Rousch Outstanding Teaching Award, Governor's Award for Outstanding New Mexico Women, Excellence in Education Award from the New Mexico Association for Supervision and Curriculum Development, and Outstanding Service Award from Project LEAD. She can be contacted at mlgonzalez6@utep.edu

Dr. Mark A. Gooden is director of the University of Texas at Austin Principalship Program (UTAPP) in the Educational Administration Department. He serves as an associate professor in that department. His research interests include the principalship, issues in urban educational leadership, and legal issues in education. His most recent research appears in *Education and Urban Society*, the *Journal of Negro Education*, *Educational Administration Quarterly*, *The Sage Handbook of African-American Education*, and *The Principal's Legal Handbook*. He can be contacted at gooden@austin.utexas.edu

Dr. James E. Henderson has served since 1992 as professor of educational leadership and director of the Interdisciplinary Doctoral Program for Educational Leaders in the Duquesne University School of Education. He served as dean of the school from 1995 to 2003. He was named a distinguished visiting scholar at Union Institute & University in Cincinnati in 2007. Prior to his most recent posts, he served 22 years as a schoolteacher and administrator, the last 13 of which were in the school superintendency. He is a senior associate in Hazard, Young, Attea & Associates, Ltd., one of the premier educational consulting firms in the United States. His recognitions include selection for the Rutgers University Distinguished Service Award, Kellogg National Fellow, and as a member of the Executive Educator 100. He received his bachelor's degree from Princeton University, and his master's and doctoral degrees from Rutgers University. He can be contacted at henderson@duq.edu

Dr. Stephen Jacobson is professor and associate dean for the Graduate School of Education at the University at Buffalo (UB). His research has examined teacher compensation, the reform of school leadership preparation and practice, and effective principal leadership in challenging schools, and has appeared in *Educational Administration Quarterly*, *Journal of Educational Administration*, *Journal of Human Resources*, *Educational Evaluation and Policy Analysis*, and *Urban Education*. He has presented often throughout the United States, as well as in Australia, Austria, Barbados, Canada, China, Cyprus, England, Germany, Israel, Mali, Malta, Mexico, the Netherlands, Norway, South Africa, and Sweden. He was president of the University Council for Educational Administration and the American Education Finance Association. He is codirector (with Kenneth Leithwood) of the UCEA Center for the Study of School-Site Leadership and coeditor (with Leithwood) of *Leadership and Policy in Schools*. In 1994, he received the UCEA Jack Culbertson Award for outstanding contributions to the field of educational administration by a junior professor. He can be contacted at eoakiml@buffalo.edu

Dr. CarolAnne M. Kardash is professor of educational psychology at the University of Nevada–Las Vegas. She received her Ph.D. in educational psychology from Arizona State University. Prior to coming to UNLV, she served as a faculty member at the University of Missouri–Columbia for 15 years. Her research has focused on two areas. First, she has examined how people's topic-specific beliefs, epistemological beliefs, and attitudes influence their processing of text, with a particular emphasis on people's memory for controversial information. Second, as an evaluator for several NSF-funded grants dealing with science education reform efforts at the undergraduate level, she has investigated the role of undergraduate research internships on interns' research skills and career plans. She served as associate editor for the *Journal of Educational Psychology* from 2003 until 2005. She presently serves on the editorial boards of *Contemporary Educational Psychology*, *Educational Psychology Review*, and the *Elementary School Journal*. She can be contacted at CarolAnne.Kardash@unlv.edu

Dr. Judson C. Laughter is clinical assistant professor of English education in the Department of the Theory and Practice of Teacher Education at The University of Tennessee–Knoxville. His research and teaching interests include multicultural teacher education and the systematic workings of race and racism in education and in society. His dissertation work focused on the preparation of white female preservice teachers to see the classroom as a site for social change through dialogue and counternarrative. He can be contacted at jud.laughter@utk.edu

Mtra. Gema López-Gorosave is professor at Escuela Normal Estatal in Ensenada, B.C., México. She previously served as professor at Universidad Autónoma de Baja California and Universidad Pedagógica Nacional and was dean at Escuela Normal Estatal. Her major research interest is educational leadership of public basic schools in Mexico. She is a member of the International Study of Principal Preparation. She is a doctoral student at Instituto de Investigación y Desarrollo Educativo, a research institution at the Universidad Autónoma de Baja California. She has published articles in *Educación 2001*, the *Journal of Educational Administration*, and *Revista Electrónica Iberoamericana sobre Calidad, Eficacia y Cambio en Educación*.

Dr. Catherine Lugg is associate professor of education in the Department of Theory, Policy and Administration, Graduate School of Education, at Rutgers, the State University of New Jersey. Her research interests include educational politics and history and the influences social movements and political ideology have on educational politics and policy. She has focused much of her research on queer issues and people, and the politics of U.S. public schooling. Her research has appeared in *Educational Policy*, *Educational Administration Quarterly*, the *Journal of School Leadership*, the *Journal of Curriculum and Practice*, the *American Journal of Semiotics*, *Pennsylvania History*, and *Education and Urban Society*. She is the author of two books, *For God & Country: Conservatism and American School Policy* (Peter Lang), and *Kitsch: From Education to Public Policy* (Falmer). She can be contacted at catherine.lugg@gse.rutgers.edu

Dr. Betty Merchant is dean of the College of Education and Human Development at the University of Texas at San Antonio (UTSA) and professor in the Department of Educational Leadership and Policy Studies (ELPS). She received her Ph.D. in administration and policy analysis from Stanford University. Before joining UTSA, she was an associate professor at the University of Illinois, Urbana-Champaign. She has an extensive background in education, having taught at all grade levels, K–12 in a broad range of cultural contexts, including tribally controlled Native American schools in the Southwest and Midwest. Her research interests focus on the differential effects of educational policies and practices, particularly for students traditionally marginalized by mainstream educational settings; school leadership for social justice; and educational decision making within a rapidly changing and increasingly global context. She can be contacted at betty.merchant@utsa.edu

Dr. H. Richard Milner IV is associate professor of education in the Department of Teaching and Learning at Vanderbilt University. His research, teaching, and policy interests are urban education, race and equity in society and education, and teacher education. He is the editor of the books *Culture, Curriculum, and Identity in Education* (2010) and *Diversity and Education: Teachers, Teaching, and Teacher Education* (2009). He is the coeditor (with E. W. Ross) of *Race, Ethnicity, and Education: The Influences of Racial and Ethnic Identity in Education* (2006). In 2006, he was honored with the Scholars of Color in Education Early Career Award of the American Educational Research Association. He can be contacted at rich.milner@vanderbilt.edu

Dr. Patrick D. Pauken is associate professor in the School of Leadership and Policy Studies at Bowling Green State University (BGSU), where he serves as graduate program coordinator of the doctoral program in leadership studies and secretary to BGSU's board of trustees. He teaches school law, special education law, higher education law, and moral and ethical leadership. He has presented and published in various areas of ethics and school law, including school violence, technology, copyright law, religion and public schools, special education, high-stakes testing, and higher education law. He has been parliamentarian of BGSU's faculty senate for 7 years and served as senate chair in 2007–2008. He is the recipient of the 2006 Faculty Distinguished Service Award at BGSU and the 2007 American Mensa National Teacher of the Year. He earned a bachelor's degree in mathematics from The Ohio State University and returned to OSU to earn a law degree in 1994 and a Ph.D. in educational administration in 1997. He can be contacted at paukenp@bgsu.edu

Dr. A. William Place received his baccalaureate and master's degrees from the University of Dayton. He was a teacher, full-time teacher association representative, and administrator for over 10 years before earning his Ph.D. in educational administration from The Ohio State University. Presently, he is director of doctoral studies at the University of Dayton and teaches research, school public relations, and personnel courses. From 2000–2002, he reconnected with the field as a high school principal. He is a past president of the Mid-Western Educational Research Association and the Ohio Council of Professors of Educational Administration. He is the 2005 School of Education and Allied Professions Teaching Award recipient at the University of Dayton. In August 2009, he was elected to serve a 3-year term on the executive board of the National Council of Professors of Educational Administration. He can be contacted at Will.Place@notes.udayton.edu

Dr. Charles L. Slater is professor of educational administration at California State University–Long Beach. He previously served as professor at Texas State University–San Marcos and was superintendent of schools in Texas and Massachusetts. His major research interest is educational leadership in the United States and Mexico. He is a member of the International Study of Principal Preparation with researchers from 12 countries. He teaches in doctoral programs in Mexico and is fluent in Spanish and French. He has published articles in the *Journal of Educational Administration*, the *International Journal of Servant Leadership*, the *Educational Forum*, the *Journal of School Leadership*, *Vitae Scholastica*, *Education* and Society, the *International Journal of Leadership in Education*, the *Journal of Adult Development*, *Phi Delta Kappan*, and the *School Administrator*. He can be contacted at cslater@csulb.edu

Dr. George Theoharis is on the faculty in the teaching and leadership department at Syracuse University working in both the educational leadership and the inclusive elementary teacher preparation programs. His research and interests involve school leadership, the principalship, equity, school reform, and inclusive schooling. His has a new book titled *The School Leaders Our Children Deserve: 7 Keys to Equity, Social Justice and School Reform*. He leads a school reform project called Schools of Promise and runs a summer leadership institute that provides professional development for practicing school administrators. He can be contacted at gtheohar@syr.edu

Dr. Megan Tschannen-Moran is professor of educational leadership at the College of William and Mary. Her research interests focus on the social psychology of schools and examining the quality of interpersonal relationships and how these impact the outcomes a school can achieve. In this regard, she has studied the constructs of trust, school climate, organizational citizenship, collaboration, and conflict. Her book *Trust Matters: Leadership for Successful Schools* (2004, Jossey-Bass) reports the experience of three principals and the consequences of their successes and failures to build trust. Another line of inquiry focuses on the self-efficacy beliefs of teachers and principals as well as the collective beliefs of a school faculty that they have the capability to foster the learning of all the school's students. She has published over 40 scholarly articles and book chapters. She earned her Ph.D. in educational leadership at The Ohio State University and her B.S.E. at Northwestern University. She can be contacted at mxtsch@wm.edu

Dr. Bruce W. Tuckman is professor of educational psychology in the School of Educational Policy and Leadership of the College of Education and Human Ecology at The Ohio State University, and founding director of the Walter E. Dennis Learning Center, an organization that provides students with academic assistance in the form of training in learning and motivation strategies. He earned his B.S. in psychology from Rensselaer

Polytechnic Institute in 1960, his M.A. in psychology from Princeton University in 1962, and his Ph.D. in psychology from Princeton University in 1963. He has authored 18 books (including editions), most prominently: *Conducting Educational Research* (5th ed., 1999), and most recently: *Learning and Motivation Strategies: Your Guide to Success* (2nd ed., 2008). He has authored over 100 articles in areas such as motivation, cognition, instructional design, the application of technology, and measurement. He is most well recognized for his theory of group development ("forming, storming, norming, and performing"). He can be contacted at tuckman.5@osu.edu

Dr. Michelle D. Young is executive director of the University Council for Educational Administration (UCEA) and an associate professor in educational leadership and policy and director of the public school executive leadership program at the University of Texas–Austin. Her scholarship focuses on how school leaders and school policies can ensure equitable and quality experiences for all students and adults who learn and work in schools. She is the recipient of the William J. Davis Award for the most outstanding article published in a volume of the *Educational Administration Quarterly*. Her work has been published in the *Review of Educational Research*, the *Educational Researcher*, the *American Educational Research Journal*, the *Journal of School Leadership*, the *International Journal of Qualitative Studies in Education*, the *Journal of Educational Administration and Leadership and Policy in Schools*, among other publications. She recently edited, with Joseph Murphy, Gary Crow, and Rod Ogawa, the first *Handbook of Research on the Education of School Leaders*. She can be contacted at michelleyoung@austin.utexas.edu

www.ingramcontent.com/pod-product-compliance
Lightning Source LLC
Chambersburg PA
CBHW022015300426
44117CB00005B/195